# You ARE Valuable

**You ARE Valuable**

Printed in the United States of
America

ISBN: 978-0-9887188-1-4

## Acknowledgements

*"This piece I have written is dedicated to Brenda who has faith the size of a mustard seed."*
**~Bergina**

*"Show faith with your work; always show love. This is for all the women in my family; I ask that God bless each life touched by this book."*
**~Carlita Sway**

*"To every person that reads this book, strive to your highest potential and be the absolute best you can be; be afraid of nothing." ~***Derrika Marie**

*"Dedicated to Melissa Wright, for showing me the epitome of love through her love for God; my angel on earth and I miss you dearly. ~***Felicitee Love**

*"To my daughter, the best thing that has happened to me outside of Jesus Christ Himself, my precious daughter, Amaya". ~***Hadassah**

*"Dedicated to the Pink Courageous Warriors everywhere; both present and in Heaven and to the many angels that support them on their path." ~**Joy Chanel***

*"Challenges pave the road to purpose. To endure one is to fulfill the other." ~**Janae***

*"Dedicated to my wonderful father resting in heaven peacefully, Kenneth C. Smith, I love and miss you dearly. ~**Karena***

*"Dedicated to my beautiful daughter, Evelyn Marie; you're the beauty that God traded me for my ashes." ~**Kharma***

*"Dedicated to my heart beats, my wonderful husband and three amazing children; you're the best support system anyone could ask for." ~**Monique***

*"This piece is dedicated to YOU; if you can relate to my story...don't change your swag, change your mind. It's God for me, He's all I need."~ **Mz. Lyrik***

*"Dedicated to my mother; no matter what she's faced her faith never wavered; she sees the Light in every situation. This one's for you!"~**Ms. Poellnitz***

*"This piece is dedicated to the One that loved me first; I cannot look back." ~**Ms. Saved By Grace***

*"Dedicated to my Fathers both Heavenly and Earthly." ~**Nekondeh***

*"I would like to thank Jesus and my Mother Audrey Hallman for all ways being there for me during my trials and tribulations and my daughter for saving my life."~**Peace B Still***

*"I dedicate this writing to South Africa, Terrance Davis (R.I.P dear friend) and Ellie Gunderson. As kindred spirits, Ellie and I, will carry your name in our hearts forever, Terrance. We love you like agape."~ **Shameka "Poetry" Thomas**,* Doctoral Student at Georgia State University

*"I would like to thank God for the life that He gave me."~**Poochie***

*"In loving memory of my grandmother Virginia Bell" ~**Sabrina***

"My contribution to this book is dedicated to my beautiful, sweet, strong, godly, 2nd mother Catherine Urquhart-Moore."~ **Shara Ashar**

"To my Father, Who knew me before I was birthed into this earth. Thank You for what You are about to do in the lives of everyone who shares in this experience. Thank You for defining our value even when we don't see the value in ourselves. Thank You! ~**Simply Stacy**

"This piece is dedicated to every girl who believes in herself, to my family, and all of those who've supported me throughout my artistic journey." ~**Spen Effect**

"For my grandmothers: Mattie L. Ridley and Catherine Loveday, who taught me to never complain and live life to the very fullest" ~**TJ Nicole**

I would like to dedicate this piece to God and my savior Jesus Christ who set me free. I would also like to dedicate this to all those who are going through life's challenges; don't give up, just run to God's open arms and He will hear from Heaven and save you in His perfect timing. ~**Veonne**

# Table of Contents

~ 5 ~

# Bergina

## *A Call From God Knows No Age*

I was a peculiar child. My mother told me when I was a baby I would play with my hands in the air; she said she always thought I was playing with the angels. Growing up, I was surrounded by family; my great grandmother was the person that impacted me the most. She taught me how to be peaceful and have patience. She had a love for God and would always quote scripture from memory. As a child,

I did not fully understand what she was trying to teach me. My great grandmother would always say, "One day I will not be here and you need to know what I tell you." I thought it kind of odd and had no clued what she was preparing me for; however, I would soon find out.

When I was four, my parents sent me to child care at my family church. We ate and played well; however, during nap time I encountered problems. Some of the children thought it was cute to throw shoes at me when the teachers left the room. Little did I know, they had a purpose that did not originate from them; they were on assignment. My parents ultimately ended up removing me from the facility.

I started kindergarten at a public school. It was colorful and I had a lot of kids to interact with; I was excited. I learned as much as they gave me. However, on the bus rides home I encountered another ordeal. A big first grade boy named James began to taunt me. I had never seen him before; he seemed to appear out the crowd of kids on my bus route. Older boys in the fourth and fifth grade came to my rescue. I was clueless as to what was going on, but I was glad the older boys defended me. One day I got off the bus walking to my sitter's house, James decided to chase after me with a knife. I ran down the street screaming. He was running and laughing. My sitter came and he went home. My parents reported him to the principal, they had a meeting but I don't recall him being suspended. After that meeting, he left me alone. I was relieved, but it was not the end of my attacks.

My soul was in warfare. I would have dreams that someone was following me. I would awaken at night calling for mom; she did not come. There were times I would try to speak, but couldn't, try to move only to feel pinned to my bed. I wondered, was I crazy? What was wrong with me? I was being attacked spiritually. Through these experiences, I realized, I had a call on my life...Christ was trying to reach me but the devil's imps were trying to keep me. They would get so close as to touch me but I would never see them; only feel their presence. Their desire was

to see me go the path of my family –
continue operating in generational curses.

At the age of 8, I gave my life to Christ but
I did not mature in the faith until the age
of 20. I had no understanding of receiving
the call, knowing who I am, and walking
in it. Upon accepting my call, I began
teaching and training others in the area of
walking in Christ. My hands are an
instrument used in dance to worship and
mark the atmosphere to the Lord. You
will have pitfalls laid before you or you
may stumble, but the key is getting back
up and remaining strong through Christ
Jesus. I have counted the cost; as I look
back over my life, I should not be here. I
am here today for someone else. I may
appear strange in my talk and walk to
some but I am a child of God seeking to
empower others along this journey.

The only question I have for anyone that
has taken the time to read this, "Will you
accept the call to go forward for what you
were born for?" Don't think it strange
that the Almighty God has a plan for you;
something for you to do that will advance
His Kingdom. God is strategic and always

has you in mind, He values you.  You are here for a purpose; the value of you is defined by YOU!

# *Carlita Sway*

## *Determine Your Value*

*It was raining so hard, I could not see the car driving in front of me. This was the worst hurricane season that south Florida had in over a decade. We were warned that Katrina was*

*building in strength and was scheduled to hit the coast later that night. My husband and I picked up the children from school and day care; this was not a good day to be outside. I was driving about 3 miles an hour, with the windshield wipers on full blast. The rain was coming down in thick cardboard sheets and the wind was whipping around the car mercilessly.*

The three babies had fallen asleep in the back seat. For some reason, my husband chose this particular moment to start another fight. He began screaming uncontrollably and trying to grab the wheel. In that moment I thought, "I am sick and tired of fighting; I have had it with this foolishness!" I started hitting him and tried to pull the wheel from his grasp. My thought was, "This was the most inopportune time for a fight, really?!! In the middle of Hurricane Katrina?!!"

"The worst hurricane season in over a decade!! You really want to do this right now?? Ok, sir.....Let's go!!!!" He sees that I am not backing down or letting up, even in this storm. In an attempt to quickly subdue me, he snatches the wheel, leans across me to open the drivers-side door and proceeds to push me out of the moving vehicle into the torrential downpour. I was getting drenched. I peeped into the back seat to see if my babies were watching any of this horrid scene and they were all still fast asleep. At that moment, I realized that it was more important for me to save their lives than try to prove I was right to a deranged lunatic. My seatbelt was the only thing keeping him from pushing me completely out of the car.

Thank The Lord God Almighty our Creator Who is blessed forever and worthy to be praised, that He had His hand on my life. In the midst of this danger the only words that came to me over and over: "The thief cometh not, but for to steal, and to kill, and to destroy: I (Jesus Christ) am come that they might have life, and that they have it more abundantly (St. John 10:10 KJV)."

That was the third and final time my husband tried to kill me. I chose not to let him have that power over me and my life any more.  I realized something very important in that moment while my dripping face was inches away from moving concrete, **God loves me**.  He sent His only Son to die in exchange for my life.  There is nothing more valuable to our Creator than our lives.  I am more valuable to my children alive, talking to them daily, taking care of them, training them, teaching them their value and worth.  I divorced my husband.  He chose to abuse substances.  His constant lack of sobriety had my home life in turmoil.  We never had enough money or resources to effectively raise our children.  We were always moving and getting help just to eat daily.  Enough was enough!

I left him, and crossed state lines with three small children, with only the clothes on our backs.  I had no job, no applications in and very little money.  I was blessed to have parents that love God and are missionaries in third world countries.  They did not want to see their own child and grandchildren in the streets.   It took me three years to build from nothing.  Today, I own our home and a newer model vehicle.  I have had the same job with an airline for over six years. I have also worked and studied to obtain my real estate license and I am a licensed insurance agent. I now have the ability to take excellent care of my children, and even go on vacations!

I am very excited to have the opportunity to impart the gospel message of hope and love. God is Love. You are loved! And you are the most beautiful, wonderful and valuable of all God's creations. When you are going through the most difficult time in your life, you are not alone. "Yea though I walk through the valley of the shadow of death, I will fear no evil, for Thou art with me. Thy rod and Thy staff they comfort me (Psalm 23)."

When you choose to accept and know your value as God's greatest creation, you can too show love and teach others their worth. Anything worth doing is not easy; there is no instant fix. When you choose a goal, work hard and obtain your goal; then and only then will you know your own worth, because you will have determined your value through your perseverance. Your God-given gifts and talents are why you were born into this life. Bless us with your true gifts. Only you can be you. You are irreplaceable.

# Derrika Marie

## Who I Am is ME...

*"I am going to the top of the mountain. You are either going to see me waving from the top or dead on the side. But you know what? I'm not coming down."*

Growing up in Denver, Colorado, I was always surrounded by love and music. I was brought up in a household where my younger brother and I were exposed not only to gospel and R & B, but reggae, rock, jazz, classical, any type of music one could possibly think of. Over time, I grew to love music in all forms; I even begged my dad to buy me a violin after seeing a violinist on an episode of Sesame Street.

I started singing in my church's youth choir beginning in middle school and sang in my high school musical, "*Grease*," at the age of 14. As I got older, I started questioning myself and losing confidence in who I was. It could have been the result of the things spoken about me by the naysayers in my youth choir circle, telling me I was not cut out to be a singer.

The shift in my heart could have come from my college experience, which was a blessing and a huge learning experience. I was constantly studying and trying to figure out what I really wanted to do with my life that was going to be somewhat enjoyable and profitable, singing took a backseat. Somewhere along the way, I got caught up in trying to please everyone (from not-so-good boyfriends and "friends" to parents and professors) that I lost myself, even though everyone thought I had it together on the outside. I had mastered the art of appearing to have it all together externally to others, but I worried constantly on the inside and doubted the gift that my Creator called me to walk in, which in my honest opinion is my voice.

After pushing music to the side for a few years to focus on other obligations, I decided after many visits, much prayer and consideration to move to Atlanta. Having been in Denver practically my entire life, I embraced the idea of moving to another city; however, fear and uncertainty crept in after being so comfortable with life in Denver.

I took a leap of faith and made the move to Atlanta to pursue new opportunities in 2010 and have not looked back since. I have dealt with some opposition from well-meaning friends and family who questioned whether or not I was "tough enough" to be in a new environment (smirk). Since moving, I have faced many more adversities, but through them all I have a story to tell, I am a stronger and more self-assured person.

It was only when I decided that I was going to be brave enough to walk in what I feel God has created me for that opportunities came along. I feel it is my obligation, my privilege, and my purpose to grow as a budding vocalist/songwriter and to help others along the way discover their true gifts and talents. I am thankful every day for the voice my Creator gave me to build up the world. It may not be that of Beyoncé, Jill Scott or anyone else, but I am learning every day to cultivate and embrace my OWN uniqueness.

My desire and ultimate goal is to let my work and life reflect that love that I experienced growing up as a child and to birth forth goodness and light in a sometimes dark and confusing world. Who am I??? I am Derrika Marie; sweet and sensitive, but also stronger and more driven than she knows.

# Felicitee Love

## I Learned To Love Me First

I was asked the question "Why am I valuable"? I paused for a second before I could answer, then I smiled because for a very long time I did not feel nor believe that I was valuable at all. I had no self-love and my self-esteem was very low. I felt unworthy, ugly, unlovable and dirty... I had been through so much in my life that by the time I reached the age of 12, I was contemplating suicide... This may seem unconceivable to some but for me, at that time, it made perfect sense.

I have been through so many storms in my life... I have endured pain on levels unimaginable: heartbreak, betrayal, abuse, teen pregnancy and domestic violence (which started in high school), just to name a few. I stand here victorious; those situations did not break me. They may have come close but I am a survivor.

I was a very angry when I was younger. I did not trust people and I felt that everyone had a motive and that most people were bad. I had been betrayed and hurt by the some of the very people that were supposed to set my foundation for relationships and love. I felt that my feelings did not matter so I kept them bottled up until something happened that would set me off and I would fight with rage unimaginable...

It is by the grace of God that I am still here and not six feet under. As I look back over my life at that time, living in the city of Chicago and the situations I came out unhurt, I am thankful. I am thankful, because I did not think that I would see the age of 14... sad I know but so true.

I was hanging with the wrong crowd, some gangbangers from time to time, doing things that a kid had no business doing. They gave me attention and I liked it, so I did whatever I had to do to fit in. I can only shake my head and again thank God that I am still here.

I looked for "me" all my life, desiring love, and looking everywhere else but never truly realizing that the first and only true love starts with self. I put on my actors face most of my life pretending to be happy, pretending to be strong and pretending to believe I was **"valuable"** when deep down inside there was a lonely, scared little girl who felt all alone.

I knew that I had to take time away from everything and build a relationship with "self." I knew I had issues and it would not be fair to bring anyone into my space until I dealt with **ME**. Yet I had to stare myself in the mirror, face and confront my issues and then build my road to happiness and I eventually found it! **I AM VALUABLE BECAUSE GOD SAID SO!**

I know that one of the many purposes in my life is to make a difference with young children and teens. I am always open and ready to do whatever is needed of me to make a difference. I want them to know that they are never alone, that they have someone who will listen and truly hear them. Someone who understands their travels and doesn't judge. Someone who understands what it is like to be young because I was too and that even young people deal with **BIG ISSUES**! Someone who wants them to know and truly understand that they are loved and **VALUABLE!**

# Hadassah

## I'll Finish Strong

*My life consisted of a series of experiences that I wish I could explain cut and dry. Though I did not understand them then, with each passing day I'm gaining a clearer perspective...that's what keeps me moving forward...*

As young child, I witnessed many violent acts within my home; my father would frequently beat my mother to the point she had to be hospitalized. By the age 4, I knew how to nurse a grown man who was recovering from a night of an alcohol binging; my dad's life experiences taught me that. By elementary school, I learned how heroin addicts shot up by happening upon my father's drug paraphernalia in the medicine cabinet.

One day, I came home after hanging out with my grandparents and could not find my mother anywhere. I looked in the closet and found her beaten unconscious and covered in blood to the point where I couldn't recognize her. My grandparents weren't too far from the apartment so my sibling and I were able to get their attention to have her rushed to the hospital.

Years went on, and I continued to witness the abuse of my mother and I felt helpless. My father left for a while and went back to New York and it seemed like things would be okay. He came back and my mother allowed him to stay with us again.

My dad would ask me questions like who'd been in the house while he was gone and me not knowing any better I told him about a man that had taken us out to eat before. My mom was beaten very badly after this, resulting in her nose being broken. My dad disappeared again and we ended up moving from the projects to a rural area.

The day that we were scheduled to move in mom never came to my grandmother's to get us. I wondered where she was. We found out on the next day that my father had shot her in the grocery store with a shot gun in her pelvic area as he was aiming for her vagina. It was by the Grace of God, my mother survived that attack on her life (No weapon formed; even if it is deployed, it won't prosper).

The day after that horrific incident, I started first grade at a new school; one of the children's parents told the students that I was the child whose mom had been shot by her father. I did not want this to follow me, I wanted to leave this behind. I was small, poor and now known as the child whose father shot her mom. I was taunted almost daily and was involved in several fights. At this point, I started to become an angry child. Though my dad was gone, the abuse continued. Now, instead of my mom being beaten by my father, my mom would beat my sister and me. It was nothing for me to be punched, slapped, cursed at, called names and hit with objects. I felt as if I had no safe haven. My grandmother did not like me because I looked like my father and I was the "darky" of the family. I got picked on at school because I was poor, short, skinny and unpopular.

For years I hated the way I looked and hated my life. I prayed that God would just let me fall asleep never to wake up. As I progressed into my teen years, I sought the attention of men because I did not feel loved by anyone else. By that time my father was out of prison and my mom had allowed him to come home and the fighting continued but not to the same degree.

My sister and I now found ourselves fighting my dad when he tried to hit my mother. He was often off away abusing drugs, alcohol and running around with other women.  My mom treated my sister and me as if she hated us and one day told me she should have aborted me.  She called me a whore before I even knew how to spell the word or had even thought of sex.  She said she never wanted girls, only boys and she treated my brother like he was a royal prince.  My grandmother would talk about how dark I was; often calling me lazy.  My sister and brother would get nice gifts, money and school clothes from my grandmother while I was left with one outfit, sometimes nothing at all.  Hard to know your value when you're so undervalued by your "family," huh?

Like my mom, my first relationship was abusive; I was 16 and he was in his twenties.  I thought this was a way of escape from the hell I had lived in for so long, oh how wrong I was.  He hit me, cursed at me, and threw things at me.

The years of fighting my dad off my mom helped me defend myself, that's how learned to fight men.  At the age of 18, I became pregnant by him and he threatened to leave me if I kept the child so I chose the abortion over losing him. I cried the entire time because I wanted to keep my child. For years I hated myself and would cry when I saw other women with children. I went through a series of relationships and friendships where I was verbally abused, cheated on and twice sexually assaulted by a people I trusted as friends.

I started going back to church; this church taught me about God but it did not show the love of God. In fact, they were kind of mean to young girls and women. I eventually learned there was more to God than just the commandments.

One day, I was sitting on my floor crying because I felt unloved and I just wanted to die. By this time I had witnessed an enormous amount of violence, my siblings and I were not getting along, we had numerous physical altercations, and I had been used by males sexually and rejected by my family. I heard this small voice speak to me saying "I love you." I sat there and I heard it again, "I love you." I laid my head down in the chair and I felt the Hand of God caress my hair and once again I heard Him say, "Daughter, I love you."

As the tears fell from my eyes, I felt this warm feeling of a hug embrace me. I began to feel restored, I started attending church more and reading a paraphrased bible. I began to learn about God loves for me and how much He cares for me.

I made a decision to no longer subscribe to thoughts and spoken lies about me, I wasn't dumb. I started putting effort into my school work, improving my grades; I then started to apply to colleges and got accepted. My story from there had many ups downs with me falling back into the world to me running back to God, my First and True Love.

While in college I met a man who I made my savior, well that was dumb because there is only one true Savior. This man cheated on me with a coworker and left while I was pregnant with our daughter, on bed rest, in and out of the hospital. He left me with debt, a child and broken heart. BUT GOD! In this time, I learned that God was a Provider, Healer and Way Maker.  What was meant to destroy me actually made me stronger.

Through it all I can say God never left me. People who know me now don't know my full story and if you met me you would never guess that I had been through so much.  What you are reading is only the tip of the iceberg.  All credit is due to God; He has refined me and has given me beauty for ashes, joy for all my pain.  I forgave my father and God allowed me to spend the last years of his life with us growing closer to each other.

We would talk on the phone every night while I was in college and I would hang out with him at his apartment.  I considered moving in with him but he lived too far from campus.  He apologized for all things he did while he was drunk and high on drugs.  He died of AIDS while I was in college.  Sad, I know but those last years of his life he was like a real father and friend to me.

I forgave my mom too; I started telling her I loved her every day and one day she started saying it back. I have two college degrees; yup! The girl that people said wasn't college material and just needed to work on assembly line. God has the final say so! God has blessed me so much financially, that I have not experienced going without in a looooong time. In fact, He has blessed me to the point that I can now bless others. I have been able to financially help all of my immediate family over the years.

Today, I am home owner and mother to beautiful, spoiled little girl. I no longer struggle with self-esteem issues as I now know I am fearfully and wonderfully made. God has restored the relationship of my family, my mother is saved. My brother, sister and I aren't at odds with each other anymore because God has healed our relationship. We actually are pretty close.

I am no longer that insecure hurting young lady but a mighty woman of God. My life isn't perfect but it's not what it used to be. God knew my end from the beginning and He promised me that my latter days would be greater and He has

not failed me yet! He will not fail you
either!  It doesn't matter where you
began, what matters is how you finish the
race.

# Joy Chanel

## In God's Joy, I Can Survive...

*So I have had my fair share of pill popping. I did not pop your ordinary Tylenol or Advil but the pill I had to swallow a year ago; the big "C" word aka Cancer. At 33, a mother, having a family, and feeling like I had my whole life ahead of me made it very difficult to swallow the acceptance pill*

that my health was potentially failing me. When I think back to that infamous doctor's visit, "being diagnosed," getting the news that no one wants to hear, being told that the stages weren't necessarily at its earliest point and that the aggressiveness meant I had to act fast. I told myself while in shock "I can get through this, as long as I don't need a mastectomy and Chemo is not required." Low and behold, the first thing that the doctor's recommended in my situation was an immediate mastectomy and Chemo...Wow...that in fact was a huge pill, I had no clue how I'd begin to digest it internally. Yet the thoughts of not being here, the 'life and death' quotes from the doctors per all of the pathology reports, made the truth inevitable.

As the pill swallowing continued, I scheduled the mastectomy, met the team of doctors and discussed the procedure which in turn meant that I was accepting the plan, along with what was the best thing for my situation. I found myself reciting almost half of the book of Psalms as I was wheeled back into a life changing procedure. Waking up but still being out of it was another pill within itself, yet as I look back I know that grace was surrounding me; I felt nothing initially. I was merely overwhelmed with the faded faces of half of my family in my recovery room. The drugs had me out of it, these must have been some happy pills for real, everyone's face was in a balloon but all the balloons were in the room.

While the plastic surgeon was talking to me it still took me a few hours to digest what he actually said. Three hours later [as I remembered it to be while on drugs] I find out that my replacement "boob" wasn't possible. Thirteen lymph nodes were removed which meant that "radiation" was now a new member of my treatment plan.

Let's fast forward to one of the hardest hurdles after surgery: removing the bandages. The first five words that come to mind "Oh! My! I! Cannot! Breathe!" When I think about my first moment alone standing in my bathroom mirror facing my "revised" self for the first time hurt more than any scratch, cut, wound, disappointment, heartbreak, or even the truth within itself.  Half of me was gone, literally, graphically, un-censored, still stapled still in an "ouch" raw traumatic state; half of me was gone.  I had to swallow the pill as hard as it was, as much as it hurt.  The reality was that God was still with me and my life still had value in-spite of the severe alterations.  I was being molded, sculpted, my testimony was forming before me, and I was granted the strength to dry my face, catch my breath, and live life even during Chemo.

My treatment plan with Chemo wasn't always a walk in the park, as I had to get used to yet another mountain of drugs.  I embraced it to the best of my ability though.  Six months of treatment that was far from mild, with low white blood counts, low potassium, 3 times hospitalized, fatigue, nausea, hot flashes, diarrhea you name it, it hit me at some point.  Yet while enduring all I could think about was "This too shall pass, my kids need me."  I knew it would be over at some point.  I received my healing in advance.  I meditated on God's Word that stated by His stripes I was healed.  I continued to live my life normally and walk in my healing.  I went to work, I went out, cooked, and walked with my head held high in my heels, wigs and diva attire like any other day.  I pressed in the midst. I pressed because God told me that if I would continue to stand on His Word and His will that my obedience to Him would result in a miraculous turn around.

Most times I pressed, not knowing that my strength, faith, and perseverance would pose as inspiration to other people in my life. It did in fact; which was a reminder to me that my living wasn't in vain. My journey/testimony would serve as an anointing, an encouragement, perhaps even a ministry to those around me.

Reflecting back on to the final weeks of radiation when the devil tried to get busy, when I was almost done with everything. Satan really tried me, he would step in with instant messages in my ear like "you cannot do this', "you're sick," "you need to give up."  On those days I would sometimes allow myself a 5 minute "Twinkie moment" where I did not have to talk to anyone, I wanted isolation and 5 second pity parties because no one in my circle of family and friends were standing in my shoes.  It sometimes made me feel indifferent and Satan would throw phrases at me in those vulnerable moments...But we all know that THE DEVIL IS A LIAR.

Even after extreme circumstances, tests, medicine, treatments, 1st and 2nd degree burns, more surgeries, and a port that is still posted in my chest; I have the glow of the Lord upon me.  I still stand, I still smile, and I still live every day to the fullest and take nothing for granted.  The enemy may have attempted to destroy me with infirmities But God.  My physicians held many reports But God!  The Pharmacy filled many prescriptions on my behalf BUT God gave me a few pills of His own; Glory, Peace, Mercy, Faith, Trust, Joy, Healing...

I am valuable because God has restored me, healed me, and turned me around.  You are valuable because I know if He did it for me, that He's ALREADY done it for you.  No weapon formed against you shall proper...

I share and conclude my testimony with you by saying this:

After leaving the doctor and reviewing a report that was three pages and filled with various underlines and notations the report of my scans show that the cancer situation has been totally turned around and transformed. All of the cancer that showed previously is showing no more. I went from doctors' visits every 24 hours to every 3 months after today. I went back to work yesterday and everybody wants to know where this new glow is coming from? I can only give the glory to God!

He is real! I am a living testimony!
I am a walking miracle! Who would have known that even after being stripped completely bare that I would have the most favor, glory, and raw beauty shine over me like never before?

Sometimes the devil will throw speed bumps in your journey because he wants you to quit, he wants your joy but he cannot have it. I am so renewed and overwhelmed with God's goodness that I have to re-pay Him, I continue to ask Him to use me, to let me give back a mere fraction of what He's given me. I am valuable, because I overcame and have a story to tell to anyone who will listen about the goodness of Jesus Christ. I continue to share my story so that others can stand as well. I am blessed beyond measures. I Am Valuable and so are you!

# Janae

## *My Side, His Side & the Truth*

*"The restraining order said I was being stalked via text, email, phone calls and social media."*

The truth is, he started recording my every move, as a safety measure, at the first sign of our being in a relationship; maybe he knew what he'd become and, not knowing if I'd fully assessed my level of damage, he decided it best to protect himself just in case.  Engulfed in my own motives and ignorant to the life he'd experienced since I last saw him 20 years ago, I never associated his desire to announce our relationship online as any cause for concern.  His request that I change my relationship status seemed odd, but I never considered the update as permanent.

Like him, a relationship with me came complete with escape routes and trapped doors for protection.  I thought I could slip in under the radar, grab what I needed, create a smoke screen of blame, and disappear like before.  Not this time though; he'd seen it before, he'd done it before; he, like I, was planning his great escape.

*"The counterclaim said I'd knowingly gave him HSV2."*

The truth is he took my tear-filled confession of having been diagnosed with HSV2 as a promise to stay with any man that accepted me.  I told him out of obligation and his assessment couldn't have been further from the truth.

Growing up in a home of domestic violence and alcoholism, I'd developed the venomous tongue of my father and, unlike my mom, a determination to never depend on a man. I craved something, but it wasn't a man. I had a need to feel needed and once that need was fulfilled, I'd quickly but dramatically end the relationship.

*"The restraining order said he created the fake profiles and inundated me with emails and text messages as revenge for breaking up with him."*

The truth is I broke up with him many times during the two months we were together, but I continued to accept his calls and to go out with him. I did not know until the court proceedings; however, that his feeble attempts to win me back were actually opportunities to gather information. I was caught with my own hook...*the need to feel needed*.

He was prepared for court. Defending himself, he'd created the case against me and, once again, allowed me to play victim after "all I'd done." Neither of us were innocent.  We were both guilty of making the people we came in contact with, the people that needed something, pay for the wrongs we'd endured.  We were both guilty of waging silent wars of revenge. Whether people needed love, understanding, money or just a shoulder, we'd give but only to get what we needed. They were trapped in a court proceeding where we were judge and jury.  Those that needed us were guilty.

No one could ever undo the molestation, domestic violence, prison, mental illness, rape, divorce, loss of a child, missed opportunities, alcoholism, financial setbacks, drug abuse, divorce, loss of a parent, false accusations, infidelity and periods of low self-esteem and depression our lives combined had endured over the years.  We didn't need to be in a relationship with anyone.  We needed to be in counseling.

In the physical, I was awarded the restraining order but, in the spiritual, I saw how all my attempts to hide instead of heal made that experience inevitable.

I no longer have the desire to lay traps; I
hope the same is true for him.

.

# *Karena*

*I Am Valuable*

I used to cringe when people would ask me about my high school days. Majority of the people I know when they mention high school, they talk of being most popular, best dressed, cheerleader or valedictorian. None of that fits me; all I can remember is being in a shell, skipping school as much as I could to avoid being teased and wondering when the four years would be over. I rejoiced in the thought that I would never have to see another school again.

Due to the fact that I was in a talented and gifted program, I did not go to the same school that the kids from my neighborhood went to. I went to a school where most of the kids' parents had more money than mine did and as a result got to wear the nice clothes, shoes and hairdos. I felt like an outcast because I did not have those things and the kids made sure every day to remind me of it. That same rejection followed me out of high school and into the work world, no way was I going to college after the shame I experienced in high school.

As a result of my school experiences, my 20's were filled with bad relationships, not loving myself, and a downward spiral of verbal abuse from people because it was as if I had a permanent sign on my forehead that read, "I don't love me, you can talk to me any way you want too and I won't respond," "by the way, I don't like the way that I look, I feel rejected, unloved and pushed to the back of the bus." I would let boyfriends treat me anyway they wanted because I was trying to get love to mask the pain.

Around the age of 25, a friend started taking me to her church, growing up, my mom would take us to church periodically but I never formed a relationship with Christ. My self-destructive behaviors didn't stop immediately because I decided to start *going to church*; it took years! Just like you cannot lose 50 pounds in a week because it did not get on your body in that short of a time, I did not immediately change when I met Jesus because I had experienced many years of rejection. I will say this, I am a work in progress. Today at 37 years old, I love myself more than I ever have and I can teach others the power of forgiveness even though there has been pain in my past. Those dreams of being a lawyer that I thought were impossible because of lack of motivation from myself or others, today I can say that I am halfway there to fulfilling that dream.

No more bad relationships love or friendships.  If you cannot value me, love me and speak kindly to me the way that my Heavenly Father does then later for you.  I have wasted too much time and destiny is calling my name.  I have a mission to let men and women know that abuse is real, it comes in many forms, and many of us have experienced it.  There is a solution and you can pick yourself up and get a new beginning.  You don't have to be a victim or be chained to your past because Christ died to set you free.  Your past pain does not determine your future; it shapes you into this beautiful diamond that can share with the world your testimony of being set free through forgiveness and love.

*Now let me tell I AM Valuable*

I am valuable today because of what I have gone through in my past.  My pain has made me valuable.  My life that the enemy tried to make me think was worthless because of rejection from friends, as well as partner relationships has made me valuable. The rejection shaped me into who I am and now I can recognize it in others and offer my testimony of how I learned to forgive. I am valuable because my Creator values me. I am valuable because every dart that has been thrown my way to cause me to give up on life and my purpose has been averted and today I am still standing.

I am valuable because I am starting to see myself the way that God sees me. I am valuable because people's opinions of me, good or bad, do not shape me, make me or break me. I am valuable because I wake up every day with purpose and destiny on my mind. I am valuable because negativity, gossip, strife and bitterness have no place in my life and I can forgive quickly and easily no matter the hurt.

I am valuable because my mind is no longer ruled by fear but by my imagination and where God would have me go to next on the journey. I am valuable because instead of being jealous of my neighbors' success, I know that God has stopped by my neighborhood and He is handing out blessings and my door is next on His list. I am valuable because I am free to love me and love others without expecting anything in return.

I am valuable because I love myself enough to close the door to toxic relationships without the fear of what others will say, and not have a bad word to say about them.

# Kharma

## A Beautiful Lie

*After the debris has settled, I sit back and reflect, "How did I end up here?" I became the chick that I would usually pity and shake my head at her in humiliation. In all of those times that I'd charge the mistress as "guilty" like the rest of society, I never thought, "Who is she and what is her story?"*

When he looked me in my eyes and told me that it was over, I believed him... Why would he lie?  He was my friend; a friend that wanted to take things to another level.  He had strings that he was attached to... That was why I told him for a year ago that we could not be anything more than friends.  I am not *side-piece-shawty* material.

Why do I need to occupy my heart or mind with the problems that come along with loving another woman's man?  I valued myself far more than that. Besides, everyone knows that the mistress always ends up the lonely one. The evidence of that truth is illuminated during holidays and her bed is often colder more nights than it is warm.

I was his friend; his genuine and platonic friend.  When he told me a year ago that he was in a committed situation that was on the rocks, I told him that I respected that and I wasn't interested in coming in between he and his wife.  I knew I deserved someone that was single and honest.

Our friendship grew for a year, he approached me once again and said that he was finished with that "situation," he went on to tell me that they were separated.  He often approached me, professing how he still wanted me in his life but he wanted more than the friendship that we'd spent a year building.  I'll never forget the butterflies that began swarming in the pit of my stomach.  Deep down, I still liked him.  In fact, I think I liked him more after we grew to be real friends; however, I meant what I said about not being the chick on the side.  I never intended to be the chick that I always felt sorry for.

We were sitting in the car, headed back to my place.  We were coming up under the bridge, about to turn into the entrance of my complex.  I looked him in his eyes and asked him if he was sure.  I told him that the last thing that I wanted was to invest my time and emotions into a situation with someone that just wanted to have a good time.  Maybe it was lust in his eyes that I mistook for sincerity; nevertheless, I let my guard down for the first time and I believed him.  That was the beginning...

With him, I allowed myself to free-fall. I thought that what we shared was really love. I knew that he was a bit of a flirt but that never ruffled my feathers. I am not the jealous type, nor am I insecure. I allowed myself to get lost into the depths of our many conversations. I loved how sharp his mind was and how he understood my perspective on so many things. I simply loved being around him. When we were together, I was happy. Our relationship had its dysfunctional phases, but when it was functional, it was magical. When we were together, I felt loved. Whenever he'd hold me, I felt like I belonged in his embrace. I never wanted him to let go. I loved the rush that he gave me, even when I was mad at him. I have never been with someone that ignited a flame in me, he did and I loved it.

I was content with the little things like riding somewhere in the car or watching movies while eating hot wings. I grew to love the small things that most people don't think twice about.

One day all of that changed. I saw him and he had two large, purple hickeys on his neck. I wanted to flip right then because I knew what it was. Instead, I calmed down and took a deep breath and I asked him, "What are those marks on your neck?" He looked me in my face and told me, "These are two bumps that I got from shaving." That was the moment the light was literally switched "on." I realized, he had been lying to me through the whole relationship. He knew I was no fool and already knew the answer; yet and still he chose to be dishonest. It was that white lie that put things into focus for me.

He lied the throughout the entire relationship. He and his wife were still together; those passion marks came from her. It took everything in me to keep me from crying and spazzing out even though I was well within in my rights to do so. That day it was all so clear to me that I was bamboozled.... I was the mistress. I was made into what I purposely said I never wanted to be: A chick that was in a relationship with a man that would never be "available."

From that day on, the man that I was so in love with became public enemy #1. I absolutely hated him for his dishonesty. I hated him for not caring about my feelings and disregarding what I told him I did not want. I hated the fact that he denied ever loving me. You do not do people you love like that. I have never hurt as bad as I hurt when the chips fell at the end of the day.

In addition to ripping my heart out, he threw shade on my name and tried to make me look like I was okay with dating him even though he was hers. To add insult to injury, he went around telling people that knew we were together that I knew of his situation and I dated him agreeing to be on the side; that was never what I wanted.

The situation became far more intense. Once truth came out, I learned that I was pregnant about two weeks later. He proceeded to act as if I did not exist and got another friend to tell me that he did not want the baby. Initially, I planned to terminate the pregnancy. Who on earth would bring a baby into a situation like this?  I literally thought that God was smoking some kind of heavenly crack that was too exclusive for Earth.  I lost a baby with someone that I was going to spend the rest of my life with almost 4 years prior to this.  An unjust prison sentence is what separates us now.

Here it is a new day and God allows a baby to grow inside of me with a man who hurt me to the core.  This baby was made out of a lie; a lie that started off as something so beautiful but nevertheless, a dirty and grotesque lie.  I did not re-think my choice until one day, the tension reached an all-time high; things got physical.  He put his hands on me; he slammed me twice; the second time was to the floor.  Being handled like that awakened something in me; when I felt my body hit the floor, I grabbed his shirt and fought back with my free hand.  In that second of defense, I managed to claw away his pretty boy quality.  I left a bloody reminder of what he had done.  He will carry the scars to remind him of that for the rest of his days.

I feel like my soul had been ripped into a million pieces. Reconstructing it would take a lifetime of rebuilding. Eight months later, I sit here spiritually leveled to ground zero. I pray to God that my mind and heart stops racing. I have never hurt on a level like this before. Dealing with the ramifications of falling in love with the wrong person is beyond overwhelming. Knowing that one day I'll have to explain this to the innocent life was that was created out of this beautiful lie.

Everyone told me to abort it. This child did not deserve to be born into a broken situation like this. I knew that at the end of the day, I couldn't do it. The haunting thoughts of hearing the vacuum literally suck life out of me disturbed me.

Lauryn Hill's song "Zion" takes on new meaning to me now; that's where I am today. Hopefully my outcome will be as beautiful as Ms. Hill's journey of motherhood. My heart holds a lot of maybes: Maybe this baby was sent to me from God to save my life. Maybe being a mother will inspire me to go even higher in my career endeavors than where I am now.  Maybe this child will be able to return the love that a part of me has been hoping for.  Maybe this baby's heart was created to hold the love that my heart has been dying to give to someone that I can trust without a doubt.  I don't know.

I am intimidated and excited to see how motherhood will evolve my life; I find comfort in knowing that at the end of the day, when I hear that cry, all the pain that I have sustained will end.  I hope keeping this life is worth it.  I am not the victim of a lie ... I am the recipient of a blessing that is beautiful.  God knows I am valuable.

# Mz. Lyrik

## I Was Created For This

*Bless the LORD, O my soul;*
*And all that is within me, bless His holy*
*name! ² Bless the LORD, O my soul,*
*And forget not all His benefits:*
*³ Who forgives all your iniquities,*
*Who heals all your diseases, ⁴ Who redeems*
*your life from destruction, Who crowns you*
*with loving kindness and tender mercies,*
*⁵ Who satisfies your mouth with good*
*things, So that your youth is renewed like*
*the eagle's*

I had a life filled with trials and
tribulations. I was very close to my father

who was very protective of me; especially since he was unable to protect me from being raped at the tender age of 7. My mother was absent during the early years of my life due to her addiction to drugs and alcohol.

My mother's illness of substance abuse caused my life to alter from childhood to adulthood quickly. I was responsible for caring for my two young sisters while my father assumed all financial responsibilities for our family, caring for us as the primary parent. Life proved to be tough for my siblings and me, due to the youth, inexperience, and instability of our parents. We moved a lot; we were raised between Las Vegas, California, and Alabama.

Although, I had the love and support of my father, aunts, uncles, and friends, I still desired a relationship with my mother. My mother's addiction to drugs and alcohol put major strain on my hopes of ever having a healthy mother-daughter relationship. I was forced to grow up and I served as a role-model for my younger sisters due to the lack of having a mother figure to assume this role.

My father tried to fill the void of a young girl needing a mother by raising me in a tough "Tomboy" manner. He put me through what I call "Man School." Although he was doing the best he could to his knowledge, this way of raising a girl would prove to be a disaster. My father told me to be independent and to depend on no one but myself. He told me I could be anything I wanted to be in life; that I could live better and be better often telling me not to grow up and be "like my mother."

Growing up in the "hood," looking around at everyday life, it certainly did not look like the place where dreams come true. In all the places I'd lived there was gang violence, murders, robberies, raping, drive-by shootings, drug dealing, you name it, it happened. I witnessed a lot of people fall victim to being a product of that environment. My father did his best to shield me from the happenings of the neighborhood but I was a part of this environment.

I enjoyed the luxuries of being "hood rich" due to the lifestyle my father provided for me and my siblings. However, it all changed quickly when my father was imprisoned for eight years; I found myself now having to activate the lessons I learned from my dad in "Man School." With a father incarcerated and an unstable mother, I found myself stepping up to the plate to fend for myself. I became a product of my environment and fell to street life; the law breaking life.

Though I felt like life had dealt me a hand of cards that I had to play I still believed in education and working hard for a living. I was involved in the orchestra and band all throughout high school; music was my way to escape what I'd faced on a daily. I used my pen to escape the harsh realities of my environment; everything that was going on around me. My peers gave me the name Lyrik; because I had a style similar to the character Lyric (played by *Jada Pinkett*) from the movie *Jason's Lyric*. I was known for writing poetry and rapping throughout the neighborhood.

I have always loved to rap; I began saving up to invest in studio time and making music with other local artists in my area (which at that time was Las Vegas, NV). I released an album independently entitled, *So Focuzed* and distributed 1500 copies. My album received great reviews and landed in the hands of prominent independent artist's label. This was just the beginning of my experiences and encounters with the Lord. Little did I know, the Holy Spirit was moving in my life and that I would one day preach the Gospel of Jesus Christ.

I was offered opportunities, but they wanted to change my image and lyrical content during a time in my life where I was not willing to conform to the request that the major labels were making. So, I remained an independent artist. In the process some life changing situations took place that forced me to pull back from doing music, and I ultimately lost my devotion to creating music. I'd lost what I thought was the love of my life, *music*, but in the midst of that I met and accepted Jesus Christ. I made Christ the Ruler and Master of my life.

I realized I was living an empty life of crime, passion, partying, and drinking, and I knew that I was here for something more than what I'd given my life over to. I accepted the Lord into my life and my desires began to slowly change. I found myself not feeling comfortable in the same places, with the same people, doing the same things. In exchange for the club I started going to the church regularly. I joined the praise team, fundraising committee, and youth ministry. I used those same gifts that got me worldly gain for kingdom building. "For the gifts and calling of God *are* without repentance." (Romans 11:29)

To me, that scripture (Romans 11:29) means when God calls you He doesn't change His mind. So, those same gifts that God had given me in the world now today I use them for the Glory of God to build the Kingdom of God. God has given me a vision to turn secular music into sacred and sanctified. He's given me a heart to use my testimony to help others change their way of thinking. I am in no way perfect, but I strive to please God and help a dying world live according to the Word of God.  I have been through a lot but I am accountable, transparent, and willing to share my story with the young, old and in between.  It is my mission to let the world know that they can be Saved and still have S.W.A.G. "Spiritual Wisdom And Godliness."  I believe wholeheartedly in Psalm 150:6 *"Let everything that has breath praise the Lord.*

I am committed to offering back to God what the devil has corrupted; our music.  I am a psalmist like David, and I know I have a heart like him.  I am not ashamed of the Gospel. I don't care if I offend man, I DO care if I offend God! I am not traditional but I respect tradition, these times call for desperate measures, I have to help save as many souls from hell as I can.

At the end of the day, if man doesn't understand you, God definitely does!  We are nothing without God and with God all things are possible.  You are valuable because God values you. You are priceless, in His Eyes and Christ paid the price for you.  He loved you first, loves

you more today than yesterday and will
love you forever!

# Ms. Poellnitz

*I Bounced Back*

        The dictionary definition of resilience is [*the power or ability to return to the original form, position, etc., after being bent, compressed, or stretched; elasticity. The ability to recover readily from illness, depression, adversity, or the like; buoyancy*].

I can definitely say I'm resilient; not by
my own strength but the strength of God.
The best way I can describe my life would
be like a rubber band that's stretched, far
and wide, yet and still it came back
together.  Let me set the stage for you...

I was created for a reason. It took me
years to realize that. God took the time to
create me and bless me with great talents.
I had no idea what He gave me until now.
I'd lived so many years of "nothing" going
on in my life; I know better now.

A man can easily distract you from
everything you want to do in life, if you let
him.  I have always been the insecure one.
I never truly loved myself.  I wanted to
love and be loved by someone but never
tried loving myself first.  That's where I
made a big mistake.  Too many women
allow this to happen to them. I did at a
very young age.

I knew the type of guy that "I" wanted.  I
detoured from that guy and tried
someone different.  This resulted in my
insecurities getting worse.  I was
seventeen and I thought that I was in love.

He lied, cheated, mentally, and physically abuse me. I ended up having three children with him; he did not help me with the children at all. Yet, I stayed. He was my "god." I'd put so much focus on him, I completely lost track of who my true God was. I was often depressed and suicidal. I knew that this couldn't be the life God wanted for me. I had to fix that problem. I knew that in order for me to get closer to God, have peace and raise my daughters' right, I needed to leave.

Faith without works is dead, right? I put up with this treatment for five years. After I told him that we needed to separate, he proceeded to put on a performance. Now, all of a sudden, he loved me so much. He wanted to change and wanted to raise our children together. By that time, it was too late. I was over him and all the drama that came with him. He was no longer my god. I took some time for me and I started to like falling in love with myself. It was like a breath of fresh air, I even began dating. My dating other people sparked a flame in him and not in the good sense. He developed a "If I can't have you, no one else can" attitude.

When he realized that I would no longer have sex with him and there was a possibility that I may move on with someone else, he took matters into his own hands. He came into my room, put his hand over my mouth, said "I'm sorry" and raped me. I had three of his children and he completely disrespected me, but for the last time. All I could do was cry. From that moment I knew for a fact that I had to move on with my life.

Was I afraid? Yes, but I wasn't alone. God had my back the entire time. I just needed to listen to Him. I did not report the rape to the police because I did not know if he would be punished. I had to take things one day at a time and give myself a chance to heal. I was able to move forward and was secure enough within myself to start another relationship. I won't go into details about this one because his purpose was to get me away from my children's father. The purpose of my children's father was to create them and to teach me what not to accept from a man in a relationship. I will never be disrespected like that again.

I have a new outlook on life now. I'm much happier than I was. I felt like I had no purpose when I was in that horrible relationship. If you're going to be in a committed relationship with someone they should add to you not take away from you. For years I coexisted in a relationship that depleted me, but I BOUNCED BACK!!!

To God be ALL the Glory!

# Monique

## Who Am I???

I am a child of God who is strong, black and beautiful. I have seen and experienced a lot yet I'm thankful. Growing up, life was wonderful. I was treated like a little princess. My parents did everything they were supposed to do and more for me. I love them so much. Entering into my teen years, I became hard headed and rebellious, not wanting to go to church; when I was born and raised in the church. My mother would make me go to church. The more she made me go, the more I rebelled. As a result of my rebellion and my mother not wanting to waiver, our relationship was going strained. I did not understand why…Why did I always have to go to church? It did not matter to my daddy because he was what we call a "Sunday goer." Daddy understood I could talk to him about anything.

When I turned 18 I became pregnant by someone I had been with since 10th grade. I thought he was the one for me; I was so happy and ready to start my family. Marriage wasn't even in my thought process just happy to be having a baby. On March 31, 1998, I went into premature labor and the baby was stillborn. The experience of losing my baby was very hard for me but GOD carried me through it. Even then, God was trying to get my attention but I was looking for love in all the wrong places.

January 26, 2000 was a very special day for me; I gave birth to a baby girl. My little princess; she was my miracle baby. I went through a process with the father of my daughter, so after the years went by I decided enough is enough it's time for me to move on with my life. I wanted better for me and my daughter.

Yet again, I was looking for love in all the wrong places. I met a guy on my job; we talked as friends on the phone and went out on a couple dates. Deep down, I knew he wasn't the person I wanted a relationship with but what happens...I ended up pregnant with my second child. I did not want another child and definitely not with him; I was so ashamed. I started getting my life together with God and was really active in church. I found myself questioning God; why does this have to happen to me? I tried so many times to have an abortion but my friends would encourage me and tell me it's not going to be that bad we will be here for you. My mother made me feel like I was straight up going to HELL and she was so disappointed in me. I felt like it was the end of the world.

One day, I prayed and asked God, "please help me get through this; You said you will never leave me nor will You forsake me." My son was born on July 10, 2004 he was such a beautiful baby. Here I am again, single but this time with two children. Rather than face what ailed me I decided to start going to the club and partying. I had fun drinking and hanging out with my friends. I enjoyed it so much; I had to go every Friday and Saturday night. There came a turning point in my life, I was really getting tired and wanted a change but I kept going.

My life changed on one Friday night in particular; the man of my dreams found me. He found me in the club of all places. He was really different from guys I'd dated. There was something very unique and special about him. We took time to get to know each other. He loved me so much, but I was really afraid to trust him because of my past hurts. I opened my heart and asked God if he was the one for me.

One Sunday morning he asked could he go to church with me, I said "No, you don't want to go to my church it's different from most churches." He said, "Ok let me see for myself." I tell you the Lord has His way of doing things. He went with me and really enjoyed the service. He told me he was tired of the way he was living and wanted to make a change in his life. God spoke to his heart and he got baptized. I thought to myself, "Oh my God, what did he just do?"

Things were moving so fast and I just could not believe it; but when God has plan it will come to past. I prayed for God to send me a man who loved the Lord first and who will love me and my kids. God did just what I asked of Him. Part of me still wanted to party after all the Lord had done for me; you know, the spirit is willing but the flesh is weak. The Lord started dealing with me heavily and the more I went to church the more I was convicted by the Word that was being preached. I gave my life back to Christ and repented for all the sin I had done.

On September 22, 2007 we became ONE; it was the best day of my life other than receiving Christ. The Lord blessed our union on March 29, 2010 when our baby girl was born. God could not have sent me a better husband then the one I have. We are walking together growing stronger in God every day.

Has my life been perfect? No, but I'm grateful for my life experiences. My life experiences have made me who I am today. Who Am I? I am a child of God who is strong, black and beautiful. Thank You Jesus, for without You I am nothing.

I say to anyone who is going through similar situations as the ones I have shared, there is no love greater than God's love. "For God so loved the world that He gave His only begotten son." (John 3:16). When everyone turns their backs on you just remember He is there He will never leave you. If you're single and desire a husband just seek God first and He will give you the desires of your heart.

# Ms. Saved
# By Grace

*Why Not Me?*

I am a single mother of two; I have raised my children without their fathers' actively participating in their lives. How, you say? God and God alone; He met every one of our needs, EVERY time.  I have worked two jobs most of my life; I was raised on the principle of hard work.  My mother was one of the hardest working women I knew; I got it honest.  I do not despise hard work, it has taught me to appreciate what I have earned and what I have been given.  The scripture, "*to whom much is given much is required*" is SO TRUE in my life because of what I have toiled through.

Life hasn't always been easy for me.  I have never been married; I have dated some good men and some that seem like they came from another planet.  I stand today, clearing away that clutter, to make sure the path I walk down is right.  My past relationships have taught me a number of things: 1) God loves me A WHOLE LOT 2) I am purposed to do something great 3) What God has blessed NO MAN can put asunder (not even me).

Walk with me if you will...
Charismatic men, well spoken, well dressed, educated men who presented the representative of themselves while I presented the true essence of myself to them which led to me being beyond hurt.

Representative 1: loving, caring, respectful – until he got to the place where he thought he could control me. He kidnapped me and literally tried to beat me into submission BUT GOD!!! Mercy said no way, NOT THIS DAY!  He snatched me from the hand of the enemy; little did I know my journey was just beginning.

Representative 2: Promised me better, showed me better, demonstrated what I thought was love until I would not allow him to disrespect me, take advantage of my kindness and sincerity.  The enemy meant for this man to take me out.  See, all the devil needs is an empty mind and a willing body; he can use you to do just about anything.  Well, Representative 2 fell prey to the plan of the enemy; he attempted to destroy me without regard for the children I'd be leaving behind.  The enemy comes to kill, steal and destroy and that day he intended to kill me physically, steal joy, peace and sanity from my babies and destroy everything connected to me.  Again I say, MERCY SAID NO!!!! NOT SO!!!!!! Touch not my anointed and do my prophets no harm (1 Chronicles 16:22).

The real point I am getting to by sharing these experiences with you is, don't make a single choice without God. Choosing friends? Ask God, being chosen by a man? Ask God. See, I did not listen to God and He stepped back and let me see what making decisions without Him would get me. For years I said God why me, then I think of Jesus on that cross, how He was beaten, bruised, spat on, lied on and cursed for my iniquities which left me to say... Why not me???

The value of you was predetermined; you have a destiny that is fully executable if you trust God to lead you. Life might have hit you hard, right between eyes, but you haven't died. Cry, scream, swing at the air, just don't give up; there's something that God specifically created you to do. Write down your dreams, no matter how far-fetched they might seem; do everything you can to live out your purpose. You are too valuable not to and did I forget to mention that someone is counting on you?

# Nekondeh

## God Does His Best With the Broken

*"I have heard divorce is worse than death. Is that true?" She asked with a straight face and since she was merely an acquaintance (whom I did not care much for anyway) I tried to respond to my co-worker with a straight face as well. I couldn't let her see the impact that the statement actually had on me. I pondered that question at home, alone; I had come to realize that I was in full blast mourning.*

Despite the constant laughing, joking, high heels and MAC makeup, the satin pillow I laid my head upon at night told the true tale of my emotional state. A quiet storm of contradictions, conflicts between love, disappointment and joy, longing, aching and rejection stirred in a pot that was boiling over, no matter how many times I attempted to lower the temperature.

Yes, for me divorce has been so much more painful than handling a death. Why? Because death is final; it brings the gift of rest. In death, over time, even the memories hurt less. When you truly love someone, in ways that you did not even know you could, those feelings don't die. They are never final. Unlike death, it is never over. When you add to that the moments when you are truly in a good place, living life, and actually enjoying it -- then, you see his face.

The moment when all the emotions you thought you had dismissed, issues you were convinced you had dealt with, come flooding back without warning. In this moment there is no time to prepare. The walls of your heart and mind have been compromised; your heart doesn't ask who's around and has no consideration for pride. Before you can even call for back up, love has made a grand entrance in your soul once again; now, the only person you hate is yourself. This has been my life for the past 5 years.

We met in high school, 1996, our senior year; we were introduced by his cousin and one of my friends. I cannot say that it was love at first sight for me; however, he would often say it was for him. At 17 and 18 years old I seriously doubted we had any inkling of what love truly was about but we knew there was something there that could not be denied. The bottom line was we immediately felt safe with one another and trusted each other.

There was a pull that drew us close to one another and for the next five years we never spent a day without each other. We married in 2001 and by then had an 11 month old son named Max. I had a degree in Communications and worked as a government contractor while he fulfilled his dream to be a truck driver like his

father before him.  We lived in a nice neighborhood in a quiet part of town with rolling hills and beautiful landscapes.
It's funny how things can seem picture perfect on paper; however, I, being the insider, knew there were flaws; not necessarily with the marriage but within myself.  I had been wrestling with the calling God had placed on my life.  I was in denial big time and had even stopped going to church in an effort to make the Voice go away, foolish, right? Yeah, I know.  Anybody who knows me can tell you that me being stubborn is an understatement.  If we know anything about the Creator of the universe we know He doesn't give up.

In 2007, I was hit by a drunk driver on 95 South with my son in the car.  The lady that hit me hit me so hard the wheels came off her car.  As my Chrysler Concord spun on that busy highway, the steering wheel twisted violently out of control and so did my mind.  In an instant I knew that my life, not my son's, was hanging in the balance.  A peace about Max had over flooded my heart and I believe God showed me he was going to be ok. Me, however, I would die without ever truly realizing the purpose for which I was created.

I had known since 6 years old that God was going to use me to preach. I would sit in the pews of our apostolic church and write sermons in my head. When I learned to read, I would barricade myself up in my room reading chapter upon chapter of the Bible. At night while I slept, my Bible would come alive in my dreams and God would show me things that would come to pass; one by one, they did. I even dreamt of my father's death; though, I told anyone but my mom.

Visions, signs, wonders and even miracles I experienced all overwhelmed me in the seconds I spent spinning out of control in that car. I tried to scream but I couldn't, which frightened me even more. Was I already dead? Then the Voice said, "Sweetheart, you cannot just make any sound. You have to make THE sound." Immediately, I screamed out "Jesus!" and the car that was meant by the enemy to be my hearse came to a crashing halt about 6 inches from the guard rail of a bridge overpass with a train coming underneath. My car was totaled, crushed like a tin can as it blew up in smoke. For a moment I was stunned and could not make the movements that my brain was sending to my nerves. I looked over at my son, who'd slept through the entire thing. He and I walked away without a bump or bruise. Overjoyed, elated, and blessed by yet another move by God to infuse my life with His love. I wanted to shout to the world the glory of God and I felt like I could take on the world. However, I did not expect to have to take on my husband.

When I decided I would pursue ministry and for once be obedient to what God was doing in me and through me, I also knew it would be the defining moment in my marriage. My husband did not really have a relationship with Christ and had not been raised knowing anything about God. Though he would attend church sometimes, when I would preach he would leave. The attack from the enemy was swift and strong. Drugs, lies, hurt, neglect, rejection, depression, home loss, everything you could imagine flooded my life; all except infidelity. I remember a prayer I prayed when I first got married, "Lord, keep us, only for each other, even me. Never let me sleep with him after he's been with another woman." I never had a desire for another man. All I only ever wanted was him. It is hard to put in to words the longing you have for the person you are in love with. Nobody else, no matter how fine or what riches they may offer, could ever replace them; no substitute. My husband had always been so good to me, sweet and very loyal. I had no reason to think he would ever be unfaithful.

The accusations started out of nowhere. This was followed by verbal abuse and downright meanness that I couldn't understand. Totally out of character, I realized I was married to a stranger. Growing up my grandmother owned a beauty salon. One memory that never left was this older woman who would say that when a man starts accusing you of cheating, and you know you're not doing anything, it's him. I also learned from the women at the shop to not go looking for anything or you'll find it. But like I said, I'm stubborn at times. One day, I went through his phone since he had left it behind in a hurry. The text messages and voicemails revealed what I had suspected but never said. Based on the messages they had not sealed the deal yet but were making plans to do just that. What hurt more was that while he was rushing out of the door to meet her in the alley beside a Wal-Mart, while I lay at home extremely sick and having just been released from the hospital that morning. Just thinking back on it now brings tears to my eyes. Yet, I did say to God that I did not want to sleep behind another woman so I'm still glad I found out.

When he returned, he swore he'd only met her to get drugs. As if that would make it better, even if I did believe him. I took him back anyway. Mainly because at that time we'd had two more children and I trying to hold onto any shred of normalcy the kids knew. The thought of giving up and tearing their world down would make me sick to my stomach; but staying in dysfunction and lies is worse.

About one month later I walked in the house from visiting my family and he was standing in the doorway just staring at me. I said, "Why are you looking at me like that and why are you acting so strange?" He took me into his arms and said, "You look so beautiful." For a second, I saw a shadow of the man I used to know; the one who held all of my secrets and who had been my best friend for over 15 years. With a smile he walked out to the car and started gathering the kids together because we were going for an outing. On the way back, while riding in the car, my husband looked over at me and said, "It's over, I'm leaving." Needless to say we had an intense conversation at home that revealed that my walk with God had basically driven him away; at least that was the excuse he was using. He did not want to get clean and did not want to live a Christian lifestyle. Nevertheless, I did not question it. I felt relief flood all over me; relief and fear at the same time.

I had only been with one man. He was my first everything. We had a great relationship, three adorable kids and the type of friendship people envied. However, none of that means anything if you do not have the glue that holds it together; that glue is Jesus. Marriage has to be built on the Rock that lasts, not the one that bling's. I had never lived alone, never raised kids alone, never even banked alone. All of a sudden the "aloneness" was very evident; except for one major Presence: the intense Presence of God. He has become everything in my life in ways I never dreamed.

This is what I have learned: Ministering to somebody based on clichés and other people's experiences is ok if that's all you have. As for me, I have a testimony of my own and this last chapter of my life is only one of them. I have endured experiences, from molestation to abortion clinics to almost being killed as a child; when I counsel someone I can speak from a place personal, deep and real, only because God has been so personal and deep and real in the story of my life.

I made a choice for God and it cost me something, someone I thought I couldn't live without. Yet here I am, living, breathing and enjoying life. My children are happy, safe and full of the joy of God.

Love is not lost, love can change forms but it doesn't die because it is His lifeline to us.  Legitimate children look like their father often in the physical but most definitely in character.  I love hard because my Father in heaven loves hard. I don't allow bitterness to creep in because it turns to hate.  It festers like a sore and stains every joy that is present in your life.  I refuse to let it stain me.  I refuse to let it change me.

Yes, this divorce, this pulling apart of my world has rocked me to my core. However, what was found at that core power, love and a sound mind makes it all worth it. So I guess it's true, divorce for some can mean worse than death. For most it signifies the end of what they thought was true love and for others it is the beginning of true life.

# Peace B Still

## No Periods Only Comma's

*Sometimes I'm reminded why I love my peace no gravel road, no melting sun, and no orange clouds. My peace is a cool sensation that enters my body from the tip of my tongue to the pit of my stomach. I have often used the term my success will be my revenge.*

*Without God I am nothing an empty shell nonexistent to mankind; I need to make a difference.*

My life is best defined by a playlist of music: *"I'll Be There – Jackson 5"* *"Three Times A Lady – The Commodores"* *"Funkin' for Jamaica – Tom Browne"* *"Hanging On A String – Loose Ends"* *"Ready or Not – After 7"* *"Slippin – DMX"* *"More Than I Can Bear – God's Property"* *"Amazing Grace – Hymnal"* *"Thank You – Richard Smallwood"*

*I'll Be There – The Jackson Five*
"You have big lips, you have nappy hair, you are so ugly, and were you adopted." Hearing that at the age of 7 hurt because when you look like your tall, dark and handsome father and your beautiful mother you wonder why others deem you so ugly. At 11 years old I shared a dream with my mother and while sharing this dream with her she told me, in French, *"C'est un monde d'hommes"* – "this is a man's world."

That statement changed my life...I did not believe her because I thought that God made this world for boys and girls.  I used to stare at her for hours because she was so beautiful; but in that moment my admiration for her disappeared until I was about 25 years old.  It wasn't until later in life that I realized it wasn't worth me being angry about anymore.

*Three Times A Lady – The Commodores*
At the age of 12 I had the body of a grown woman but I was still very much a child. My mom taught me how to fight; I found out why at the age of 16 when a boy tried to rape me in high school.  I remember it like it was yesterday, it was in the Future Farmers of America (FFA) area of the school.  This area was all the way at the end of a hall past the gym.  When he pinned me down and I saw the look in his eyes, I thought to myself "Bridgette it's either going to be you or him; this is NOT a man's world, "don't let him get you."  I then thought to myself, "This is worth going to jail for, do it now!"  I proceeded to head butt him and used my pencil to the stab him in the neck.  He yelled and a lot of people came running out of the gym. I thought to myself, "Where were they when I was yelling?"  (GOD only knows).

I can laugh at it now, but I still remember how it felt to feel helpless and angry at the same time. After this incident my ego changed, I went from flying under the radar to a "mess with me at your own risk" attitude. I believe that little girl still resides in me for protection from the big bad wolf.

*Funkin' For Jamaica – Tom Browne*
I did not meet my first real friend until high school; the day I walked in the girl's bathroom and saw everyone picking on a girl name Angel. Angel was picked on, beat-up at school. I later found out she was also abused at home. She was my first friend. Angel never had any peace and I thought it was my duty to make it stop. Remember, I still had a chip on my shoulder because I earned my bad girl badge for almost killing a boy during an attempted rape. After I went off to college Angel and I lost communication. She became pregnant for a very abusive man who later killed her and he got off with self-defense; she was 5ft and was 6'3...

I couldn't save her from him. I later realized it wasn't my job too. **Life**

**Lesson:** *you cannot interfere with God's plan (testimony) God's plans are not like your plans.*

*Hangin' On A String – Loose Ends*
Ahead of me lies a journey that my past had prepared me for; I just did not know it...

He was a red neck tall skinny blond haired blue eye white boy from the other side of town who wore dirty boots, wrinkled jeans and polo shirts. He comes up to me and says, "Hey girl I'm going to marry you." My immediate response was, "like hell you will white trash, I don't know you." I meant what I said too; but when a man loves you and wants you he will go to ends of the earth to get you. He did just that! He will have the patience of Job, (not like the job that pays the bills but Job in the bible).

He would come to my track meets, when I would race cars on the back roads; he was always there. I was not his experiment; he wasn't mine. He loved my dirty panties; I know because he used to wash them for me. He told me he would always take good care of me and I would never want for anything. He often told me in absolute confidence that no other man would love me the way he loves me.

*Ready or Not – After 7*
Sunshine and rainbows turned into deep dark clouds smothering you until I could not breathe.  On April 24, 1995 at 7pm I received a call at home that my husband of 6 years was dead.  The man that taught me the importance of having a covering, the man who showed me the order of love; he loved me first, that in turn made it easier for me to love him; he was gone. Life seem to spiral downhill drastically at that point; at 6 a.m. on April 25th, I lost our child.  I sat in the middle of my living room drenched in my own blood and that of our unborn child, emotionless, hurting physically and completely dead spiritually.  The stress from the grief I felt caused me to miscarry.  The entire Adams family was wiped out in 24 hours.

I no longer felt like "me" so I decided to shave my head, I slept with my doors unlocked, sometimes wide open and armed with weaponry.  I felt as if everything that was good to me was gone. Yea, many thought I was crazy, heck, I did not care, I felt crazy, I felt like there truly wasn't much life to live left in me. I merely existed. I buried my husband Saturday April 27, 1995. Everyone cried I did not. Everyone wanted to hang around I did not. Everyone wanted to talk I did not. I left because he wasn't there. I loved my husband with all my heart and soul; he was a funny man who would give the shirt off his back and never cared about money or things. At this point, I was too confused, hurt and angry to want to stroll down memory lane.

**Life Lesson:** *Everything isn't always what it seems God has a way of giving you a testimony.*

*"Slippin – DMX"*
I quit my job, moved in with my parents, and found myself living in a room that had ants that I made my pets, I named, The Adams Family: you know, "*They're creepy and they're kooky,*" at that time in my life, that theme song fit me perfectly. Funny enough to think about the ants even added to my journey; they were

strong, but the cold killed them; no matter what though, they always returned in the spring.  Reading this today, I have to laugh at myself.

Even though I was in a place of confusion and pain, God still saw fit to make good on the promises my husband made to me. With the money he left me, I purchased my first church's chicken and put my cousins to work, hoping to make a difference in the community; in myself.  I learned through this experience that you cannot mask pain; you have to deal with it.  I was still a mess; I started drinking a lot, my parents began to complain so I moved out.  I got a job working for Nortel Networks and moved to North Attleboro, Massachusetts.  I got off the plane, with my bald head, cowgirl boots, and sunshades...ooooh that wind was cold. The cold, healthy advice and Toni Braxton showing up on the scene prompted me to grow out my hair.

*More Than I Can Bear – God's Property*
I wish I could say it was all on the up and up from there, but I did not' write this to lie to you (there's enough crap out there

for that).  One day I got a call from my mom asking me to come home; I went to visit and my dad was skinny he went from 250 to 150.  I asked him what was wrong with him, my mother says his drinking has caught up with him he is sick and won't go to the doctor.  My dad had only been retired for only 6 months.  I arrive home, the next day my daddy and I take a ride to the store and he tells me he has Cancer.  He goes on to tell me he doesn't want treatment and for me not to tell my mother.   I told him to call me when it's time and he then went on to do the "daddy" thing and give me some of his good advice,  go back and live my life and stop drinking because it's going to kill me. He could smell the alcohol coming out of my pores.  Houston was hot and makes you sweat, I was drinking all day; I could afford it, I was a lush.

A couple of weeks passed I'm back in Massachusetts drinking and partying- the day after the phone rings- it's my dad- "It's time for you to come home."  I flew home, sobered up for 3 days to help my daddy make his funeral arrangements.  I was careful to make sure I notated every intricate detail of his life; he was a Mason, who practiced Islam then converted to a Baptist serving as the Sr. Deacon and Treasurer at his church. He was also a mentor for men in a leadership program within the city of Houston; not to mention a great husband and father. On the last day of making his arrangements he told me not to come back to the hospital because he was going home. I left and came back later that night; I should have listened to him because all I remember now is how he was gasping for air, my mother was crying and my uncles telling him they were there for him and its ok to go. I wish I'd never gone back to the hospital, I wish I'd listened to my dad...

My daddy died on August 8, 1997.

**Life Lesson:** *Obedience is for your protection; heed to it.*

*Amazing Grace - Hymnal*
I decided to relocate to the city of Atlanta; for no other reason than to party of course. I was fully engaged in SIN (Self Indulgent Nature) - I went from wanting to save people to not helping them at all

evening my own mother I haven't mentioned my sister. I took partying to a whole new level; now I was sleeping with a guy that was fun to "kick it with" when I was drunk. I ran 10 miles a day to keep myself distracted; I had a routine.

My runs, ran me into my next phase in life…I felt sick; thought I may be pregnant by my sex boy toy. I told him, "If I couldn't have my husband's child, I don't plan to have yours." I don't know if you all have noticed by now, but that chip that was on my shoulder years back had turned into a hard exterior that consumed me. On May 8, 1998, a + sign brought me to my knees and I'd asked God to forgive me for all I'd done. I heard in a still small voice, "*It's time for you to stop you will die if you stay on this path.*"

An infant saved my life: TiMani Victoria Olivia Roberts was born on December 19, 1998.

**Life Lesson:** *You are not who you were, you are not who you are and you are not what you will be until God is though with you.*

*Thank You – Richard Smallwood & Vision*
At this point in my life, I knew I needed
Jesus, but I wasn't completed dedicated;
however, three years ago that's when it all
began to change. I met a young lady at a
new job I'd started; she brought Jesus to
my desk EVERY day for lunch. Every day
she brought me Lunch, the Word of God.
God started chipping away at the
hardness had me bound; I forgave where I
once was determined never to forgive. I
forgave my daughter's father, who was
now my ex-husband; this made my
daughter's life much easier. I don't have
hate in my heart anymore; I no longer
drink to mask my pain.

I was greedy, selfish, sinful, hateful,
neglectful, and downright mean. But God
still love me and He brought me through
it. I'm a wealthy woman who is
surrounded by people who love and
respect me. I'm not sick from all the
alcohol abuse because He has made me
whole. I don't have hang ups or dirty
laundry and I don't pride myself on
anything that I have done wrong. I miss
my earthly father and I have built my
relationship back with my mother. I have

hope again and I have dreams, something so simple is very valuable because I am a natural born dreamer.

I was born with a specific purpose, I am valuable.  I thank God every day for my peaceful life because 24 hours is enough time to do the right thing.  When Jesus decides I am out of time; I hope that I have fulfilled my responsibilities and made my Heavenly Father proud.
No period= never ending

Only Comma's=continuous with God in charge of your life

Live the life God has blessed you with and rejoice in the swamps as if it was a nice clean pool of water.

# *Poetry*

## *Permission to Cry Furiously: Surviving Death and Depression*

*....naturally, I keep everything bottled up inside. The problem with that: it is completely unnatural to keep everything bottled up inside.*

I crashed into my 20s; skydived into them without a parachute. I hit the ground on various occasions, only to get back up, and do it all over again. The thing is, I never gave myself a chance to process each fall. I went through milestone after milestone—and did not give myself a chance to celebrate nor grieve.

**20 years old.** I was a brave junior at Spelman College who adventured off to study abroad and dwell in Cape Town, South Africa for a whole semester.  No one in my family had ever went to a four-year university or even lived overseas; I was a first-generation, a pioneer.  It was a blessing and a burden, to trek through such uncharted territory.  In South Africa, I met lifelong friends, kindred spirits, poets, artists, professors, heroes, and warriors--it was astonishing.  I stayed up long hours, danced at night clubs, got high off of marijuana for the first time, skipped classes, slept in church, partied all night long, and fell into a strange lustful love story with a Zulu man.  I thought life was great.

Just days before my 21st birthday, we went on spring break.  We rented a car, drove over five hours to another part of South Africa, on our own—no adults, no permission slips, no parents checking in—just our grown selves. We had adventurous activities prepared for every day of the week, including: walking through billion year caves, Ostrich riding, bungee jump off of the world's tallest bridge, and hiking down a mountain slope to the Indian Ocean.  It was five of us, all good friends, but three of us were really close friends.

I must have needed alcohol at every meal even Smirnoff-Vodka at lunch.  My good friend Terrance and I got into an intense debate about the alcohol beverages. He believed that I did not need to drink all of the time.  I believed that I did.  We went back and forth over right and wrongs. Eventually, we stopped talking on the trip.  The very next day, we hiked down the mountain slope; such beautiful scenery.  The best part, we weren't even afraid.  The sad part was, Terrance and I were still not speaking to each other.

We spent hours on that slope, which led us to a breath-taking beach. The beach had gorgeous white waves, crashing in on huge boulders and rocks.  It was amazing. We all sat there and day dreamed, wondering how all of this was created, and by whom was the artist.  Terrance and Ellie went to put their feet in the water and stood there taking pictures. Suddenly, death shadowed us. A gigantic wave swept Terrance and Ellie off their feet. Ellie was able to catch balance and survive, but Terrance could not. He was carried out by the wave's undertow. I stood there, watching. Watching, as the wave swallowed my friend. He was never seen again. It took rescue three weeks to find his body. The worst part of it all, I never got to apologize to Terrance about the alcohol.

The fact that we never made up haunted me in my every thought. We stood on that beach for hours, waiting for rescue to come. It was the first time I felt God, but also the first time I could not believe God. How could God do this to such a good person who was only 20 years old? I felt betrayed. I felt deeply pained in the very pit of my soul. The rescue crew arrived and this white, blonde guy in a surfing suite approached me with ocean on his face and tears in his eyes, he asked "Do you believe in miracles?" At that very moment, I broke down and wept. This was the first time I had ever seen death up close, staring me in my soul. I kicked, screamed and cursed the heavens. I could not fathom telling Terrance's mother that he was gone. How could I? He was the only child and this was his first time out of the United States. I wanted to die at the thought of it all.

That moment, life happened like a flash of lightening. I was scared of water for a long time after that. I woke up in pitch soprano screams at 3 AM. I was scared to take showers, for fear of the water swallowing me. I hated life, I hated that I survived, I hated that I could not explain life or death. My birthday was three days after Terrance's death—I turned 21 years old and I aged painfully.

Ellie and I were so broken that we moved around Cape Town, South Africa without souls; merely existing, but not feeling. It was truly the worst moment of my life. We were given counseling and a therapist; his name was Clint. He was one of the sweetest South Africans ever. For the first three sessions, I did not speak; we sat in silence. I stared at the floor; I stared out of the window. I felt trapped, not by his office, by life and death. There was nothing Clint could say to me that would make me feel better. I hated these sessions, leaving these sessions, going back to my dorm room, looking in the mirror, I hated that I survived. Clint called it "survivors-guilt" and "survivors-trauma"—and I called it, emptiness.

I managed to finish my semester in South Africa. I guess I blocked Terrance's death out of my mind. I artificially tried to move on. When I left South Africa, I read The Alchemist by Paulo Coelho for the first time—finished the whole back during my flight back to the United States. That book walked me through my journey step by step. It healed certain parts, but the deeper parts of my journey—I hid them—from the world, and worst, from myself. Those hidden parts, I decided, did not deserve healing.

**21 years old.** I shaved all of my hair off my head and walked around like a female-boy for the longest. I decided that no amount of make-up or earrings could make my soul like pretty. When the study

abroad ended, I moved straight to
California.

I spent the 2$^{nd}$ semester of my junior year
at the University of California-Berkeley. I
had no expectations. I just showed up to
the Berkeley campus and blended in with
the hippies. I found myself at peace
among the people who rocked peace signs
and hot pink hair. It felt like that they
could understand death. I loved how they
floated aloof, yet spoke in theory.
Berkeley, that street of Telegraph and its
homeless professors, healed parts of me.
I sat out on the grass, smoking grass,
letting them play music to me on the
acoustic guitar of my soul. I dressed in
mismatched colors, became a vegetarian,
grew my hair into a huge afro, walked
around bare foot, sang songs off key in the
middle of the street—I felt a piece of
home, a piece of peace.

As classes started up, I met a male
transfer student. He was tall, dark, and
handsome. I wasn't drawn to him, nor did
I ignore him. I just watched us, as we
flowed into this solid friendship. Next
thing I know, he became my boyfriend.

We walked slowly together, laid down together in our dorm beds, got high together, and talked about nothing. We were polar opposites and our opposites attracted each other something serious. While I don't remember things like a first kiss or first anything—I do remember him always being around. We grew together, graduated together, loved and suppressed each other. It was a love and loathing story. At the close of the semester I gave up my acceptance letter into Princeton University to stay with him. I gave up everything, I don't know why—but I did. When I think back sometimes, I wish hadn't given up everything.

**22 years old.** I went back to Spelman to finish my senior year. I hadn't turned 22 years old yet, but I was planning a huge birthday bash with my Spelman sisters. I got some of my coolest female friends together and we hired a stripper! Girl........that stripper was SEXY!!! Whew! I got so wasted and danced the night away so much, that I woke up on my couch in a state of panic. It was 10 AM and no one was home. The house was trashed, friends were gone and I was alone. Suddenly, I felt completely overwhelmed. I sat on the couch in fetal position, holding myself really tight. I felt a spirit come over me—and it was dark. That was the very first day of my deep, dark, depression.....

I spent my entire senior year at Spelman, battling with depression. I was in denial for quite some time. No one could understand why I went from extremely happy to such a strange slump. I did not understand either—all I knew was that every day felt like I was walking through hell. All of the memories of the past crept back into my sleep. I was afraid of the dark and afraid to go to sleep. I felt so low, I often cried all day and all night. I pushed all of my friends away and existed in solitude. Melancholy was my new friend. Nothing looked the same; even the color yellow looked black. I did not want to go to church, pray, write poems, or speak at any engagements. I became an empty soul, lost, and stuck in trauma. Depression hurt every part of my body. My arms and legs trembled in grief.

Terrance's death hunted me like a ghost of the past that I had not put to rest. I went through several anxiety attacks and even had to go to the hospital on several accounts. I was placed on Zoloft to deal with the hormonal imbalance, in hopes that it would release endorphins to the rest of my body.

During this deep, dark, quiet depression—I had a few key friends who left my side and kicked me even further down. On the other hand, I had a few key friends who helped me choose survival. Taylor and Jumeka signed me up for counseling services. It wasn't hard to talk to them, since they battled with the same depression, too. My long distant boyfriend at Berkeley, even he stayed with me through the hardship. Sometimes, I think he stayed because he loved me; other times, I think he stayed because he was depressed, too. Either way, we pulled off a long distant relationship for quite some time, while ignoring the signs of incompatibility because misery loved company.

By the time spring semester of senior year crawled around, I was still wading in the trenches of depression, begging for relief. I remember going to this Ghanaian party with two of my Spelman sisters. We got drunk and partied the night away. The problem with that is: when a depressed person gets drunk, the emotions fly out. On the way home from the party, my friend and I got into a terrible argument, yelling and cursing at each other. So, at the red light—I jumped out of the car. Now, why did my skinny-self jump out of a car at 2:00 AM in Atlanta, GA, leaving my purse and my cell phone in it? How utterly, stupidly, DUMB! But again, depressed, drunk people make the worst decisions—well, at least I did. I had no way to get a ride back to Spelman, nor did I have any contacts to call someone to pick me up. I was alone in Atlanta, with club cloths on, walking down the street, bound to be kidnapped and never seen again.

My fear led me to run to this local McDonalds. I went inside and asked to call my boyfriend, who was far, far, away in California. I called him and asked him to call someone to come pick me up, without calling my parents. It took over an hour, but someone came to pick me up from the McDonalds; that was the night that I *realized* that I need to get my life together. It's one thing to KNOW you need to get your life together and it's another thing to REALIZE that you need to get your life together. That was the night that Sky introduced me to meditation. I was always afraid to meditate. I tried once before, during the beginning stages of my depression, and the thought of sitting that quiet for so long, made me want to vomit.

However, Sky encouraged me to try again. He told me to not be afraid of myself and to see the quiet as a door entrance for love to come in. Three minutes into the meditation, I broke down and cried. In that meditation, I felt a loving presence carry me back to the day that Terrance died. That loving presence, asked me to open the eyes of my heart and see that the waves had been calmed. That loving presence said, "*Terrance is worried about you, more than you need to be worried about him.*" That loving presence also said, "*Terrance cannot be at rest, until you release him."* It had never dawned on me that I had never released the death of my friend, Terrance.

A whole year later—I had not grieved or processed his death. I was ignoring it. I was letting it pile up inside. My anger and rage was slowly creating a tsunami inside my stomach. I had never given myself permission to cry furiously. Senior year drifted onward—I started meditating every day and found rest at night. I stopped smoking weed and taking Zoloft and focused on my deep breaths, instead. I was revitalized not only by meditation, but by working on my senior thesis, making up with my friends, adopting a stray cat named Snookie, and meeting up with some other survivors.

One day, I woke up and stopped taking the depression meds. I looked at the bottled and gave it a kiss—and kindly placed them in the trash. I still needed help through the journey and the meds helped me balance a little, but I was at peace with no longer needing them. I vowed to never need those meds again because each day—I would DECIDE to wake up a survivor.

**THE LESSON:** It's amazing how one decision can transform your life! My battle with depression was one of the hardest slumps of my life. It made me realize that depression is a spirit—a negative spirit that thrives on isolation. So, the more isolation you are in, the harder you have to fight to make decisions. You have to be delivered from depression. You have to decide to wake up a survivor. And it may be one of the hardest decisions one could ever make because when you are depressed, your mind convinces you that you are surrounded by death.

No amount of therapy or medication can make you overcome it alone. It takes an intentional decision and a strong dedication to devote to your inner spirit to survive depression. I am convinced now that the only reason that I did not die in my depression was because deep, deep, deep down inside—I secretly wanted to live. I just had to regain the strength to give myself permission to live because when you are depressed—you feel that you do not deserve life or anything that gives life, such as food, good friends, dancing, smiling, conversations, or even waking up.

I had to give myself permission to know that I truly deserve all of these things and so much more. I am happy to say that not only did I conquer depression and release Terrance's death from my spirit, but I also graduated from Spelman College, *cum laude* and my senior thesis won the Scholar-Activism Award. From that moment forth, I have DECIDED to NEVER be that low again! And no doubt, there will be hard times and struggles, but knowing that God found me at my low point changed my life. Now, I meditate and pray all of the time; it honestly is the source of my strength! It is my daily bread!

In closing, I wanted to let you know that it is not by accident that you are reading this excerpt about depression! Realize that you are only breathing because something deep, deep, deep inside of you wants to survive and refuses to die. As life comes and hard times come, learn to process.  And of the biggest life lessons of process and healing is: GIVING YOURSELF PERMISSION TO CRY FURIOUSLY. The best gift you could ever give yourself: is Permission to Cry Furiously.

# (RE) SEARCH

*(we) searched. it took 3 weeks to find his body.*
*lifeless. we stood on the shores of south africa.*
*empty pockets. barefoot. starring into an ocean*
*that did not have an answer. our souls full of*
*questions.*

*(we) searched. it took 3 minutes for the water to*
*flood his lungs. his was the only child. Like*
*jupiter. he tried to swim, but the waves were too*
*massive. his eyes were brown. full of salt water*
*and tears. no goodbyes to friends. our hearts full*
*of inquiry.*
*(we) searched. it took 3 seconds for his eyes to*
*match ours. in the deep in. no lifeguards. just his*
*brown body in the indian waters. fighting for*
*oxygen. fighting for a hand to pull him back to*
*earth. no one knew how to defeat the universe to*
*save him.*

*(we) searched. stood on the shores drenched in*
*pitch soprano yells. screams like knives. too*
*much water. could not find his hands in the tide.*
*(we) searched. and screamed. and cursed the*
*air. and fell to our knees in humility. why?*
*(we) searched. for our closest friend. only 20*
*years old. sociology major. studying abroad.*
*first time overseas. trapped under seas. gone.*
*just like that. how?*

*(we) searched. for a mother's only child. first*
*generation. college student. lived in his*

*georgetown university sweat shirt. ate peanut*
*butter out of the jar with his fingers. a smile the*
*size of the sun. a heart as warm as the moon. a*
*laugh as loud as birth. couldn't find him.*
*(we) searched. looked deep into the crevices of*
*the oceans. prayed to the sand castles. asked the*
*seashells if they knew his hiding place. no one*
*knew. not even the star-fish or the seagulls.*
*(we) searched. yelled at police officers.*
*threatened rescue men. aimed our fist at the life-*
*guards. You freaken team of pathetics. how*
*could you know C.P.R? did not you learn how to*
*save lives? where is he?*
*(we) searched. heard his mother's tears in the*
*phone. heard her say the word, no, 20 times in a*
*row. she in america. us in africa. her son in*
*another life now. miles a part. the last hug from*
*her child was 2 months ago at the airport*
*departure. flight 189 to capetown. no, no, no,*
*no, no....*

**Shameka Poetry 2011© All Rights Reserved.**

# *Poochie*

## *Name Please???*

*My name is Poochie. Poochie is my childhood nickname; given to me by my mother. From my understanding, I was a very fat baby, but if you see me now you would say no way! I chose to carry this name as an adult and in my business as well. It's been with me all my life. It describes me. Many come to conclusions about my name; but the fact of the matter is it's mine, and I love it.*

I am a Savannah girl who found her way to the "A" – Atlanta that is! I am self-employed and as a child whenever someone asked me what I wanted to be or do when I grow up I would always say I am going to work for myself. At that time I had no idea what it would be. I am a natural born hustler and I mean that in a good way.

I have been in Atlanta for 16 years, I am a Nail Technician and I own my own nail salon. I have been in my shop for 12 years. I take my business very serious, and I treat it as if I was on someone's job clocking in & out. When I first moved to Atlanta it was very hard. I can remember sometimes going to my car and crying while I was at work, wondering if I would make it, thinking, "can I do it?" The first apartment that I moved into had no furniture. I was sleeping on the floor scared, hoping I was going to make enough money to pay the rent when it was due. It was like starting all over again, but I knew it was where I wanted to be.

I am a firm believer that you can do whatever you put your mind to. I was willing to tough it out, and that's what I did. You have the key to your destination just put it in the ignition and drive. I love what I do, but yet & still there is so much more to me. I never take my situation for granted and I treat everyone with equal respect. I am well aware that there are some people who don't know what their calling is in life. I am so grateful that I learned of mine early. If you pay close enough attention to yourself, you will definitely find your calling too; often times its right there don't overlook it.

I continue to ask God to keep my mind fresh, and full of ideas that I can follow through with. I am a praying person, a seeker & a researcher and one thing I am big on is loyalty, I take that to the heart. I am blessed to say that God has really placed some cool people in my life along my journey. Another thing that fuels my journey is when I'm challenged by someone and tell me I cannot do something that drives me into full force to get it done. Again, I can do anything I put my mind to.

There is so much I want to do.  I want to go on a vacation, I have never been on a real one, I have a passport that I have never used, but its ok, I love what I do & when you love what you do it's hard to get away from it.  Sometimes I sit back & say, "Wow, look what I have accomplished."  I know where it comes from, God above.  What I have accomplished may not look like a lot to the average person, but it's a lot to me.

I have learned in life that we should take responsibility for our actions and not blame anyone else for something that we played a part in.  Why do we settle for less when we are worth so much more?  I have made up my mind that I am not going to settle for less, because I am more.  I am so excited about my future. It cannot be anything but good; I am not going to accept anything less.

I am the type of person that learns from other people mistakes.  I am not saying I am perfect, I am far from that, but at this point in my life I want to do the right thing.  I know where I am going and I know where I want to be.  There is something really big in store for me I know it, I feel it.  Watch and you will see...

Find your value, today.  God created you to do something different, be something different, and achieve something that has never been done before.  You will not know the value of what you bring to the table until you realize the value of you. I'm grateful that I know who I am and Whose I am.  Catch hold, the world is waiting and looking out for you to shine through!

# *Sabrina*

## *The Mirror*

*"You never know how strong you are, until being strong is the only choice you have."-*
*Unknown*

When I look in the mirror, what do I see? Am I proud of the person I am today?  I am imperfect, I have physical flaws that I try to cover and hide.  I have weaknesses that I try to conquer.  My heart has been broken several times, which has caused me to question my worth. I have made some bad decisions and have had to deal with the consequences. There have been several tests of my faith and I have not always passed. My eyes have cried many tears due to disappointment and weariness. I have endured some harsh realities; yet - I am proud. I am still standing! With boldness, I declare God's best. He is calling me to fight and to continue to move forward. There are lessons that have to be learned. I will never stop believing in the awesome power of the God I serve. My heart still has joy even though I do not have complete understanding. I can still worship and jump for joy in the midst of uncertainty. How? Because I am holding on to God's unchanging hand.

I grew up in a Christian family that taught me to have a personal relationship with God. I believed in miracles at a very young age and was in awe of God and what He meant to me. Even though I strayed and attempted to fill the void in my life with other people and things, God was always there waiting for me to return to Him.  He promised to never forsake me and to this day, that holds true.  I believe that I am pleasing Him as I walk out this thing called faith.  It is necessary.

The world around me is rapidly changing. There is a culture of violence that is alarming and I worry about the children and their future.  Who are they looking up to as role models?  My hero was my grandfather; he was truly one of a kind with a big heart.  He loved God tremendously and he spread love to all who encountered him.  When he left this world, it impacted many; I too want to leave an impact.  I want to be able to love without restrictions or fear of rejection.  I want to completely be myself.  I think change will only come about if we freely and unconditionally love one another.  It's easy to point out differences and another's flaws, but we should learn to focus on the positive in one another.  I do believe there is treasure within us all - we just have to love a little bit harder to access it.

The word *worth* is described as "having value or importance" and "excellence of character." I did not realize the importance of self-love until I hit rock bottom in a relationship that I thought would last forever. I considered myself a very confident individual until I gave my heart to someone who did not value it; I felt unloved and dishonored. Trust is vital to any relationship and once lost, it is hard to regain. I became very reserved and unhappy with my life and the choices I made. I turned to food for comfort and gained weight. Why did love hurt so badly? What was wrong with me? I would just cry when I did not know what words to pray.

I lost hope for my future and felt stuck. It took a prophet speaking over my life for me to realize that God allows second chances; that my life was not over. I had a choice and I had to get up and make a decision to leave behind the heartache and reach toward the heavens. I had to understand that God was bigger than any problem that I would ever face. I realized, without the rain, I would never truly appreciate the sunshine. I grasped the importance of knowing my worth. When that happened, I never allowed another person to validate me. I am who God says I am. I am unique and wonderfully made!

My inner circle is full of people who challenge me, notice my talents and abilities and allow me to grow. I'm surrounded by people who dream big dreams and only want to go higher. No one will ever stop me from dreaming. I love and accept myself; God has a plan for my life. My Light within must continue to shine.

# *Shamiah*

## *I See Grateful…That's My Eye's View*

*I see things at different angles than most. When it comes to my life as a whole, my interpretation of it is truly one of a kind. I think before I react, research before I assume, and most importantly, I do rather than say.*

Sometimes it's a challenge to do things out of love, joy, and sincerity. I strive to go beyond society's standards, stretching my mind to unthinkable things –things that most people wouldn't step out into or give thought to. Every day God blesses me to see, I challenge myself to be a better woman than I was the day before. I embrace opportunities that are presented before me.

I was not born with a silver spoon in my mouth, hot food wasn't always available, and my neighborhood did not consist of picturesque landscapes, big houses, and pretty fences. I grew up on 63rd street Parkway -- Chicago, Illinois, where I was born and raised -- Cook County! I saw a lot growing up in the city with my siblings and cousins. Laughter comes out of me because it amazes me how God kept His hands over us in the midst of all the mess we engaged in and the mess that was happening around us.

During my teenage years, I went through some hardships that I felt were unbearable. I struggled with low self-esteem and had no confidence in myself. I lost my identity, trying to keep up with other people. I struggled with lust, sex, and boys; this drew me away from God. I cried out for help when help arrived I was too blind to recognize that the Help was right before my eyes.

The toughest to bear out of everything I had been through was developing a firm relationship with my mother.  My mother and I never saw eye to eye and I could not understand why.  Why I always felt pain and neglect from her?  Why we couldn't have a mother-daughter relationship that was shown on TV?   I felt she loved my younger siblings more than she loved me.  Why, after all the letters I wrote to her, the conversations that took place after those letters, was there was still emptiness?  I loved her so much and for that love not to be reciprocated was agony in my heart that dragged for years; however, I kept fighting! As a child, as a teenager, I kept praying -- asking God to make things better and He did.  I recognized the strength God gave me at such a young age.  I used the gift of strength that He gave me to the best of my ability and my mother and I are closer and stronger than ever before today!

I have learned to recognize when I am wrong and take the necessary steps to getting right. No, I am not perfect, but the value of me is found in knowing Someone who IS perfect and accepting His love for me in spite of my imperfections. The value of me is not determined by my hair, nor my size, the scent I wear or the color of my eyes. I have seen some things, been through some things and yes, I still have plenty more to experience; however, I try to see the light in every situation I face. I strongly encourage others to do the same; it makes life so much easier.

Through every situation I have endured, I have gained strength to realize and apply the concept - "I am MORE than conqueror." It took a long time for me to see God's love for me and just how good He is to me, but now I know. I am more grateful today than ever before. God has allowed me to touch people's lives by doing poetry. I will never forget the day when my mom looked me in my eyes and told me "Mya, You are my Shero!" That stands strong in my heart today, and motivates me to keep pushing. Given the struggle my mother and I went through, the meaning and significance of those exact words, "You are my Shero" that is more than enough confirmation as to why I... Shamiah Patrice Am valuable!!

The change that I personally would like to see take place in this world is a much stronger and more serious approach to education, especially with my generation in particular. I am 20 years old and I don't believe the life I have lived is in vain. It is my hope that our teachers, facilitators, ministers, school boards, mayors, parents, grandparents, everyone would take the future more serious.

To me, it would be a wonderful thing if everyone could stop thinking about themselves and money, and start promoting education and long term careers, rather than sex, quick fixes, money, and drugs. Am I willing to make that change? Most definitely! Why? I am enticed with being the voice or the catalyst so to speak that my generation needs to hear. I am all for positive change, and I feel that the more courage and motivation is being bled out, the more people it could affect...which would essentially lead to change.

# Shara Ashar

## I Am She...She Is Me

*Finally, I see the way God pursues*
*embraces, entreats desires, is passionate,*
*overwhelms and displays His love for me.*

As a little girl, my mama bought me a
name card from a kiosk in our local mall
as a present. I was so excited because I
was receiving a gift and I was finally going

to find out the meaning of my name. When I looked at the name card it read "Princess." I thought to myself, this has to be a joke? The people at the mall lied to get some money. "Princess?" for a shy, quiet little girl, from a small city, with daddy issues and low self-esteem, yeah right!

My name is Shara, when scrambled it is the same as Sarah. The name Shara and Sarah are one in the same, the same amount of letters and meaning. Shara, as well as, Sarah means Princess, yet the first thing that came to mind when I think of the name Sarah is the word Barren. Barren: *to be incapable of reproducing; unproductive; desolate.*

I have been married for almost 11 years and praying for children, enduring smart remarks, teasing, crazy looks and hypocritical actions because I haven't had children yet. For example, "Everyone is getting pregnant except, Shara", "What's wrong with you because we know it's not him," "If I have another baby I'll give it to you to raise" or the worst comment ever "Ya"ll (f-word) every day and still cannot have a baby?"  Not to mention the moments when my husband would become frustrated and I had no means to ease his angst.  Sometimes, people take for granted, that what may come easy for them may be harder for another.

Meanwhile, my family members and friends have had multiple children in the years I have been married.  All the children in my life call me "Auntie" and though I love it, I am looking forward to becoming a mother and hearing a little person call me "Mama."  Having a child of my own will be one of the greatest experiences of my life.  God continues to hold my hand through this whole life changing process.  Can you imagine waiting years for God's promise to come to pass?

I began to look over my family history; how my little sister and I were the only children in our immediate family and my mother was also an only child.  As a matter of fact, my family became smaller because many marriages did not produce children.  I had to go back to the foundation of my existence to get through this season of my life, my faith.  The Word of God truly provides everything we need to live and succeed in this life, even with all its storms.  I started looking back at women in the Bible that faced similar journeys as my own.  I started with Sarah; she was passed childbearing age but God gave her a son and before He gave her a son He gave her a promise.  Then there's Rebekah, her husband interceded on her behalf and she bore two sons, Jacob and Esau and let us not forget Rachel and Hannah.  You see, God doesn't want me to sulk; He wants me to be encouraged and to encourage.  When I think of these examples the question comes to mind, "Is there anything too hard for God?" Certainly not!!! If He did it for them, He can do it for me.

One of the fruits of the spirit is long-suffering; funny right??? Yea, I feel like I have been suffering a long time, but when I get all in my feelings about it I'm politely reminded of how Jesus suffered for me. He suffered and yet I am reaping the good fruit from the pain He endured.  Needless to say, I build a bridge and get over myself QUICKLY.  However, I know now that God has an intended purpose for this "princess" all I have to do is be patient, trust Him and follow His plan for my life.

If you're reading this, I encourage you to do the same.  If life seems to be handing you more than you think you can bear, trust me lean on God, He's right there. God wants to help you, God loves you, He wants to get to know you and He wants to show you love.  Don't stop moving toward what's in your heart, consult God, make sure it's in line with His plans for your life then go after it FULL FORCE, no one can stop you as long as you stick with Him.

# Simply Stacy

## "They Call Me Lady Girl..."

I never knew the significance of the name that my Grandma Becky endeared me with until I got older. **Lady**: *A woman of superior*

*social position, one of noble birth.* **Girl**: *A female child; a person's daughter.*

I have to be honest; I did not grow up believing that I was beautiful, special, or needed. My life consisted of major losses, pain, anger, bitterness, forgiveness, hurt, low self-esteem, suicidal thoughts, major stumbling blocks, that intended to throw me off course.  The life I led was a far cry from the fairy tales Hollywood movies and reality TV tells today; however, I can confidently say that as a result of all that I have been through, my life is all the more worth living.

I'm proof that strength comes from trials; I don't look like what I have been through and that is all because of God, telling me my value. I'm a priceless commodity in His Eyes; all that I have faced wasn't in vain but for an intended purpose; I see that now, today. I will not sit here and say the road to finding value in me was easy and no, I did not achieve it alone.  It took a series of unexplainable trials, tribulations, and processes to get me here.  Would I go through them again if I had to do it all over? I have to be honest and say no, I really wouldn't want too, but thankfully my life's process isn't up to me. I smile at the thought of where I'm headed now, because of where I have come from.

I was born to my mom at her 28th week of pregnancy and she was 31 years old (considered advanced maternal age); this was in 1978. I weighed two pounds and eleven ounces; as soon as I was delivered I was rushed to neonatal intensive care. The doctors advised my mother that because of my "*condition*" I may not make it. They told my mother it was their recommendation that she leave me there because I would be dead in a few hours anyway... amazing huh? God said it, "*the power of death and life are in the tongue.*"

My mother did not receive the doctor's report, she told them to do everything they could to care for me and where they couldn't God would (I'm thankful for a mother who had enough faith and love to want to save my life). I overcame what hurdles the doctor's spoke initially, but they continued to report all types of ailments that I would develop as I got older. They said I would have brain damage, mild retardation, unable to speak properly, immobility, you name it and they said it.  Once again, my momma believed the report of The Lord.  He told her that she'd bring forth a healthy child, able to stand on her own two feet regardless of the condition I was born in.

I did not learn to walk like most kids.  I attended physical therapy every day; the therapists and my parents were hopeful that one day my legs would be strong enough to stand on, they never gave up hope.

Hope came one night in 1982 at *Bethesda Bible Way Church*, in Petersburg, Virginia.  It was my family's church, grandmother, cousins, sisters and brothers, we all went there.  Every year, the church would have revival and yes, we went...EVERY night, to EVERY service.  At the end of each service the pastor would conduct an altar call.

One night my mom and dad carried me down for prayer. The pastor that was teaching that night, was named *Thunderbolt Jackson* (laughing to myself, I am not making this up) anyone that went to *Bethesda* at that time knows this to be true. It is my understanding that he was called "Thunderbolt" because his voice was powerful, he spoke with STRONG conviction; honestly, he did not need a microphone. Anyway, she brought me down for prayer, her petition was for my healing; he prayed for me. What happened next, the doctors REFUSED to believe, he told her to put me down and go to the other end of the building. I walked from the altar to my mother at the other end of the church, no one was carrying me, assisting me, or holding my hand (well I take that back, I believe Jesus was) but nonetheless I defied the odds that day.

Little did I know, that was God's way of saying, "*I have plans for you and no matter what you do or what happens to you, they will come to pass; you ARE valuable to Me.*" I continued to overcome what was spoken over me: I made the honor roll almost every year in school (so much for the brain damage), I articulately conveyed my thoughts clearly in oral and written form (speaking properly) I was a cheerleader (so much for being immobile) God did it! I wish I could say life was all butterflies and roses from then on, but God had to develop character in me.

Another stage of my development began when my mom died; I was thirteen years old when she passed, suddenly. I grew up immediately; it was just me, my brother and my daddy. My daddy worked tirelessly to keep the burdens he struggled with off of my brother and me. Faith was shaky; but present; God never took His Hand off of our lives. I cannot say I understand why it all happened the way it did, but I can say that had it not happened we probably wouldn't have grown to become as close as we grew to be. I had to feel my way through life, leaning to my own understanding (so you can imagine how many of those scenarios played out). I thank God because He was still with me, directing me, even when I thought I was doing my own thing. He valued me enough to never leave me unprotected, even though my actions warranted me to be.

At the age of 18, I attempted suicide. My mother was dead, my dad was locked up, and I felt like I had no one to turn too. I'd convinced myself that life was unbearable and I couldn't take another second of it, but Mercy said NO!  I said it before and I'll say it again, boy am I glad my life's process wasn't up to me.  God knew, I did not have as long to wait for my turnaround as I thought; so even when I did not want to hold on He held on to me.

My daddy came home; it was a challenging year, but a good year because through that time, God strengthened the relationship between my daddy and me. At the age of 19 I decided to move away, try my footing on my own.  I made a lot of decisions without God's guidance that He was still able to work out for the good of me.  I have to tell you, Romans 8:28, *"And we know that all things work together for good to those who love God, to those who are the called according to His purpose"* has been real in my life, for sure.

I was growing into a lady; but still very much a little girl.  I ran from everything that *looked like* it wanted to hurt me, I affirmed myself through the validation of others and I made choices, that people judged me harshly for. I had an abortion that same year; I did not need the judgment and stones thrown at me by people, because my own guilt and condemnation was doing well enough on its own. However, I can proudly say today, that it ALL WORKED OUT FOR MY GOOD!

At the age of 20 a friend had a real and honest conversation with me, she wrote me a letter and in her letter she said, *"Stacy, God loves you; far more than you love yourself and no matter what you do, He will never stop loving you. He wants to forgive you too, all you have to do is ask."* It was that day, that I made a decision to allow God to have His way in my life. I asked Jesus into my heart. Life was still life; but now I had a Covering, I had a guarantee from God that no matter what I faced, He'd be with me, loving me and He'd work it all out, all I had to do was trust Him. I had to remind myself, that what God means by *working it all out* will not always fit my definition.

God proved me once again, here recently; through the loss of my daddy in June

2012. It was in this process that I believe I gained the most growth. My daddy was diagnosed with Cancer in late 2011; his condition worsened and he was told in April 2012 that he had 30 days to live – BUT God – He knows higher, He knew higher. God gave me and my daddy an opportunity to spend every single day together, some days were better than others for him. We got a chance to talk about things, that honestly, had he not been in this situation we probably would have never discussed.

We did a daily Bible study, cried together, and God even blessed me with the honor of watching my beloved daddy take his last breath (60 days longer than the doctors reported). I was able to honor my daddy, by preparing his program and coordinating his home going service. I thank God for His wisdom, because He showed me through my father's life and his passing that no matter where you come from, what you've done or what you've been through stick with Him and He will honor you. My father left this earth with honor and dignity, peacefully and most importantly reconciled with the Father.

Today, I can proudly say, I believe in my heart, mind, and soul that I AM VALUABLE!  Is life perfect? No.  Do I still have problems? Yes.  But I have hope, faith, and Joy to see me through and thankfully the Joy I have isn't driven by how I feel.  I am *Lady Girl* a person's daughter who grew up to be a woman of superior social position.

# *Spen Effect*

## *Eternal Flame*

*"I am the hottest of all hot fireballs"*

I am the hottest of all hot fireballs. My personality can best be described as a flaming meteor. My energy soars through any roof up into the heavens and the character I possess instantly causes one to fall in love with my adoring charisma and southern hospitality. I am power. I am beautiful. I am authentic. I am what young, black, and inspiring looks like. In the poetry scene my peers have labeled me "*The Flame*" but on the photography scene I am "SpenEffect." This insane passion for the arts has taken over my being since the tender age of six and I knew I was destined for something "MORE"; something beyond the big country outskirts; something beyond the city of Columbus, Georgia.

From the beginning, I always knew I would have to fight for what I wanted in life. Life has not been a bowl full of sugar or honey for me. The eldest of four children, being the only girl, I was always fighting. Whether it was to defend my honor, maintain respect, for my brothers or the people I loved, for some reason, I refused to be bullied or taken advantage of regardless of who they were or whatever authority they held. My father died before I was born and my mother and I never developed mother-daughter relationship. I was (and still am) a granny's girl. My grandmother is an amazing, strong willed, never give up, fight for what you believe in till your body is numb and blue type of woman. She is who I have patterned myself after and she is the sole reason I know what hard work is (my shero.) I credit her for the animalistic creature I have become in regards to going after what I want full force, no speed bumps or stop lights ahead. With this type of backing and support behind me, how could I fail? Despite the fact that I have no father or mother figure giving me the boost I have always craved for, Elizabeth Reddish has given me more than any one girl could ask for. I am grateful that she is mine; that her legacy will live on through me as long as I walk this earth.

Reading and writing has always been an important factor within my existence. Escaping in a story was my get a way. Creating my very own story felt like summer vacations and as a young girl, I just knew I would be the female version of Stephen King. I took pride in my craft and as a child I believed in myself because my value as a person was drilled into me early. No matter how much value my grandmother instilled in me, it took years for me to finally look myself in the mirror and say "Spen, you are beautiful too." To look past and accept that I have never had the straightest teeth has always been a challenge for me growing up. I was picked on and called so many names there's literally nothing any human can call me today that would surprise me. Dark skinned girls were not considered "pretty" growing up where I'm from. So imagine me a dark skin, nappy headed, crooked teeth, and short girl growing up in the country. I will say at the least it wasn't a kid friendly episode on Nickelodeon.

Writing and photography became my escape; my way of releasing any anguish and emotional havoc that I held within. At first, I wasn't good at verbally expressing my emotions. I became a mastermind at bottling everything bad inside until a bad situation would cause me to erupt or until a hurtful remark would literally break my heart. I eventually realized that there will always be someone who doesn't accept me or my appearance; that I cannot allow myself to be broken whenever this occurs. I couldn't allow one more tear to fall because in actuality some people take pride in seeing someone cry versus someone smiling. This is where spoken word came into play. Being that I have always had an insatiable appetite for the arts I gained the courage to actually speak in front of a live audience. One day I was driving on the highway and it hit me, "*If I can memorize songs on the radio of people who I'll most likely never meet, I can memorize my own work, words that have actual meaning and importance to me.*" To know that I had the power to freeze time with the click of a button through photography fascinated me. I learned to look beyond the image standing in front of me when it comes to shooting in frames. I taught myself that it's more than pressing "flash." Photography is about capturing precious moments and or memories in time that we as people can never get back but with a picture have a reminder they will never forget.

My very being is valuable because I know there is no one like me. My voice is one of POWER and REASON. Today I, am unafraid of ridicule, opinions or the popular crowd. I am the voice of every black girl who wants to make the most out of her life; who wants the whole world and a bowl of Cheetos hot fries. I had no mother or father role model and I haven't allowed the street life to trick me out of my freedom. I know my poetry has saved my life over 98 times and the lives of at least 98 other women and men on the east and west coast.

I am positive my poetry has helped several women hold their heads up higher, love themselves a bit stronger and accept all the pain which makes them beautiful and all the more grateful. One person at a time is how I expect change to create change. Change one person's insight on life and the change within them will prompt them to change the person or persons surrounding them. Of course change doesn't happen overnight but one day at a time and a motive to do better in life itself change cannot be resisted.

Being the flaming fireball that I am has driven me in more ways than ten. No matter what I'm my biggest cheerleader; however my toughest critique. I never give up on task; I see it all the way through even if I'm not totally satisfied with my performance.  I am a role model to many students, peers, and elderly and the belief that I will succeed no matter what keeps my flame from never burning out!

# *TJ Nicole*

### *Speak Love*

*A man's stomach shall be satisfied from the fruit of his mouth; from the produce of his lips he shall be filled.  Death and life are in the power of the tongue, and those who love it will eat its fruit-Proverbs 18:20-21*

Children are often told to slow down. Enjoy being a child as long as you can and don't grow up too fast.  They are warned about the stressors of being an adult -- demanding jobs, difficult decisions, and the never ending stacks of bills. When I was 15, I couldn't wait to become an adult; to make decisions for myself, and have the freedom to go where I pleased and do what I wanted.  More importantly, I wanted to get away from the man that abused me for most of my life.

When I think of my childhood, it is mostly a blur.  There are a lot of blank spaces, probably my mind's defense mechanism against the painful memories.  What I wish to share with you, I remember well--

I was a freshman in high school.  I was very gifted, and I had just started a magnet program.  My mother was adamant about me going into the program even though it meant that I had to be bussed over 30 miles away from my home. Like clockwork, the bus picked me up at 6:00 AM each morning and I returned well after 5:00 in the evening.  I learned how to complete as much homework as I could during the two hour commute and most days when I arrived home, I was exhausted.

One afternoon after a long day, I passed out on the couch in the living room. My book bag was still on my back; I was that tired. I must have been sleeping really hard because I did not hear my step dad come in. I was half asleep when I was ripped off of the couch and thrown face first into the stairs. *"How many times do I have to tell you not to sleep on the couch?! You have a bed, use it! This is my house and there are Rules...Rules you will follow!"* He continued to yell at the top of his lungs, cursing and threatening me. He grabbed me and threw me again; this time I slammed hard against the stairs, not quite at the top. I scrambled the rest of the way up the stairs, crawled into my room and locked the door before he could reach me again. He pounded on the door, still yelling, but I would not unlock the door. I was breaking another one of his many House Rules.

I sat on the other side of the door, terrified. For the first time in my life however, I was not afraid of him. I was afraid of myself.  I was so angry; I felt like I had what it took inside of my heart to kill him.  For years, he had punished, cursed, threatened, violated, and abused me. My heart was racing and my mind was spinning. All I knew in that moment is that I wanted him dead.  I prayed to God and asked Him to release me, or even better, destroy him. I began throwing over the furniture in my room, tearing apart everything I touched. I destroyed my own bedroom; punching and kicking the door and walls. This continued to the point where I had no energy left in my body and eventually passed out on the floor in a pile of wreckage.

When I came to, there was another knock at the door; this one was soft, gentle, and somewhat cautious.  *"Tiff, are you in there?"* My mother had finally gotten home from work. She pleaded for me to open the door but I couldn't. I did not want to see her face.  As far as I was concerned, this was all her fault; she married a horrible man and I was trapped in a living hell because of her.  I hated him so much and a piece of me hated her even more.  A mother is supposed to protect her child.

After what seemed like an eternity passed, I unlocked the door and my mother entered my room. She stood there with the look of shock on her face. It was a while before she spoke, as she had already started trying to put the room back together.  After a long silence, she asked what happened.  Her low voice cracked as if she was holding back tears.  But I knew tears would not come...I had never seen my mother cry up until this point in my life.  I sat there motionless; I could not speak.

Days passed and I did not speak to either of them. Despite the many times she asked me to tell her what happened that afternoon, I wouldn't. There was a lot I never told her. This day went into the vault with all the others.

The next few months were quiet.  I avoided my stepfather as much as possible.  When I was around I gave him icy stares to let him know not to mess with me. I think he knew that I had snapped and if given the opportunity, I would bring a lifetime of hurt to him. I wanted him to hurt in the ways that I had all these years. I wanted him to experience the fear that he had inflicted upon me.

Then it happened.

He was diagnosed with Cancer and I was shocked. He began radiation and chemotherapy right away. The Cancer had attacked his throat and he nearly died when fluid filled his lungs. His stay in the hospital was a long one. His body became weak and frail. After having a trach tube inserted into his throat, his voice became a raspy, pain-filled whisper. Time continued to pass and his condition was not getting any better.

One night I watched him closely; he labored to breathe, his body was hooked up to a bunch of tubes, and machines were beeping and buzzing nonstop. I felt a huge amount of guilt. I felt as if he was lying in this hospital dying because I had asked God to punish him. Many nights I had prayed for him to die. Now I found myself praying for God to save him. No one deserved to suffer like that. No matter what he had done, I knew that he should be forgiven and healed. I went to his bedside and combed his hair. It had become matted and tangled from weeks of lying in one spot, without even the strength to lift his head from the pillow. He looked at me with the kindest eyes I had ever seen in him. I assured him that he could get better, but if given a second chance, he would have to make changes in his life. He could no longer speak hate.

My stepfather made a full recovery from Cancer. Today I reflect on the many valuable lessons I learned early in life. Through the hurt and pain, I learned the power of forgiveness. I learned the power of prayer from the sadness and grief I experienced. One of the most important lessons that I learned from all I had faced was that God loves me and placed me here on this Earth to demonstrate the power of unconditional love. And from out of darkness shines the brightest lights. I also learned that one of the most valuable possessions God has given to me is my voice.  With the gift that is my voice, I choose to always speak LOVE.

*Veonne*

## Transformed By Grace

*And do not be conformed to this world, but be transformed by the renewing of your mind, that you may prove what is that good and acceptable and perfect will of God.* Romans 12:2 New King James Version

Have you ever desired the life of someone else, because their life seems glamorous? As people, we find it natural to desire the success of the wealthy – however, we fail to consider all the obstacles they had to overcome to reach the polished, finished product. My

name is Veonne Lightburn and I have been in the same place. As a child, I always desired to be the next successful, millionaire – but I never understood the process of being successful. I assumed if you pursue your dreams, they will land in your lap with little troubles. At the age of 21, I realized that even though I haven't walked into my first one million dollars, I am still successful because God has changed my life through the various circumstances that I put myself into. Why am I successful? I was delivered from the homosexual lifestyle – a lifestyle that not many **choose** to leave.

As a child, I was always the center of attention – if you did not give me attention, I would find the attention elsewhere. Being the only child had its benefits and downfalls, you could say. "Why did I crave attention?" What else would a child desire when their father is in prison? I needed a father in my life, a father to love and protect me. The lack of protection soon came to haunt me. At the age of seven, a young man exposed his body to me. When I was exposed to his body, he told me to do things that I have never done before. He revealed to me a book of sex positions that was engraved in my mind. The house grew quiet, and my mother knew something suspicious was going on – was her child being molested? She rushed into the room and found her seven year old daughter in her underwear, untouched and unharmed. My mother snatched me from this young man that she babysat, and cried with devastation in her spirit. Who knew that this one incident of being exposed, at the age of seven, would leave me sexually curious in my pre-teens?

Being raised by my grandmother for most of my life had its benefits. My grandmother was there to council me and raise me in the things of God – despite my circumstances; yes, I was a church kid. Some years passed and my love for God grew while being in the household of my grandmother.  Then, my dreams came true, my father was released from the prison's pit. He was free from prison one year before I entered middle school. I was excited about this new journey that I have dreamed of for years – I finally had my father in my life! I moved in with my mother and father expecting the picture perfect family; I would later find out the opposite was going happen. Living with my father was great, he loved me and was willing to do anything to make me happy – however, all I wanted was time with my father. Gifts and surprises came every day, but we only got to spend time together on Sundays. I began to "eat my pain away." As I continued to eat out of depression, I began to find attention elsewhere. I began to go online to meet friends and eventually, I would find an interest in online dating to ease my loneliness. I went through a lot of identity crisis, trying to fit in where I was accepted.

There was a point in my life where I became overweight and my father began to buy me boy clothing. As I dressed like a boy, boys became my company – and eventually, I began to think like a boy. My desires began to grow for women as my addiction to pornography grew and as I surrounded myself with perverted teenage boys. These desires conflicted with my church foundation.

I always found myself going back and forth in my mind when it came to the bisexual lifestyle. Considering that men betrayed me in relationships and my childhood, I began to grow distant from the desire of men. I would go to church, repent, and attempt to date a young man in hopes that my heart would change – but this only made my pain deeper. After four years of identity crisis, battles with marijuana, pornography and lust, my desire for God rose from its dormant dungeon.

I remember the day that I sat in my room, with the feeling of emptiness and loneliness – I knew what I was missing, but I wasn't sure if I was ready to make such a commitment. I sat on my bed, scrolling through Facebook looking for someone to talk to, because I felt God wouldn't want to talk to me. A little chat box came up, an old friend from middle school messaged me (we did not talk for years, so this was surprising). As we began to talk, I told her that I missed 'the old Veonne', the 'pure Veonne'. She replied to me, "Well, tell me about you, as though you were the old you." As I began to tell her my life, as though my present never existed, I began to feel the bounds of condemnation and lust fall off. I began to feel free; I began to feel the love of God again. Tears began to roll down my face and I experienced a new love, my first love – the presence of God. That night, I rededicated my life back to God – in the small bedroom that I once considered my 'secret place.' This secret place has officially become the altar where Christ visited me and turned my life 180 degrees.

Rededicating my life back to Christ wasn't the easiest thing to do – when temptations were around every corner, so I had to let go of all the friends and influences that wanted me to continue that lifestyle. I isolated myself so that I could know more about God and his love for me. That summer, I enrolled in a Christian college and got accepted! I now have my associate's degree towards Christian Ministries! I have been transformed inside and out – and what people may think is impossible, I have seen God do a mighty move in my life. He transformed me from dressing like a stud, to reflecting a mighty woman of God. Genesis 1:26 says that I was made in God's image, and I can truly say that this scripture has come to fulfillment in my life. I have been set free from the bondage of depression, and all the glory belongs to God! I can do all things through Christ who strengthens me! Since leaving the homosexual lifestyle, God has used me to set the homosexuals free from the bondage of confusion! I have been used to deliver them, through the power of Jesus. I have also been used to minister to young girls and young women stuck in broken situations bounded in insecurity and lack of identity.

So why do I consider myself valuable? I have been used to set the captive free. I am one of the few people who have been set free from the choice of homosexuality. I am 21 years old, and I am still a virgin. I am one of the few women who have decided to stay pure until marriage. Even in the midst of peer pressure, I am glad that I can say that I am pure. What seemed impossible for man is possible for God; God has set me free. God is using my testimony to set people free – and I will not be ashamed because there is freedom in the power of my testimony. I am here to present the Gospel of Jesus Christ, and God will change the hearts of the bonded men and women who deal with rejection and lack of identity. I will be the one to stand up and I will see the change that God will do.

If you are struggling with homosexuality or bisexuality and you want to be set free this is your chance. The bible says that if we confess and believe that Jesus is Lord then we shall be saved. Do you believe this today? Do you believe that Jesus can save you? There is power in the blood of Jesus! He is alive today and He is here to heal and restore you! Repeat this: "*Jesus, I admit that I am a sinner. I have sinned before you, and I want to be set free from sin. Today, I repent, and I accept you into my life as my LORD and SAVIOR. Which means, I will let you live through me. Even though I am not perfect, I will strive to be more like you every day. I believe you are the son of God, and I believe that you died in my place, and you rose again that I may have eternal life. Your word declares that you have given me the keys to the Kingdom*

*of Heaven, the keys to bind and loose –
whatever I bind on earth shall be bound in
Heaven whatever I loose on Earth shall be
loosed in Heaven. So right now, I bind every
demonic, perverted mindset that I have
and I cast it down into the pits of hell. I
cancel all plans of retaliation from the
enemy. I loose love, power, and a sound
mind. I take hold of the mind of Christ, and
I put on my armor for war. I commission
my angels to go before me. Your word
declares who the Son sets free is free
indeed, therefore I believe, by faith and
speaking this declaration, that I am free -
because there is power of life and death in
the tongue! I am free and delivered! Amen!*

Remember that after being delivered
from bisexuality or homosexuality, you
will be tested and tempted. However, the
word of God declares *I can do all things
through Christ who strengthens me.* So
walk in your victory today – you are new
and redeemed! Live in victory because
God has made all things new for you!

Don't meditate on the past, He has chosen
to forget the past things that you've done
– you are literally new in His eyes. Renew

*your mind* daily because that is where the battle will take place. Believe you are new and walk in it!

# *Nita*

## *From Victim to Victorious*

*"I'm not defined by my circumstances; I'm refined because of them."*

I was a woman who wore many hats: daughter, sister, mother, aunt and friend to many.  I wore my smile proudly, despite the pain I might have had brewing inside of me.  See, I learned it's not phony to think yourself happy, in spite of what is transpiring around you; when you do that it's a sign of growth, a sign that you're trusting God to fight for you.  I worked hard, started working at the age of fourteen.  I was blessed with many gifts, gifts that God Hand delivered to me.  I was a cook by nature, baked pies with closed eyes, I also knew how to sew; that came in handy when money was low.  I enjoyed doing both very much; let me share with you a little bit of my story…

Life wasn't a fairy tale for me, I became pregnant and was married at 17; to a man I thought loved me, but instead he wanted to control me. He used his masculinity to bring me under subjection to his insecurities; I was his punching bag. I thought he loved me and that he would change, so I stayed and we had another child. Now, I'm a mother of two married to a man who only thinks I'm good enough to beat on and sleep with...enough couldn't come fast enough, but not without trial and error first. My self-esteem was tattered and torn, I found myself a woman scorned; however, this hurdle that seemed bigger than me I would overcome. I had to maintain for my children; I desired better for them. I left their father, thank God with my life spared and I was able to move forward.

I moved forward, maybe a little too fast; word of advice when you're overcoming the adversities of life, allow yourself time to heal. Just because the sore has a scab on it, doesn't mean it's healed totally. I hadn't dealt with those demons I'd acquired while with my ex-husband and moved into another relationship. This man had everything good looks, charisma, educated, and confidence. We both came to the relationship, loaded down; he was the father of two girls and I was the mother of one girl and a boy. We dated, he showed me things I'd never seen and another amazing thing that captivated me was that he loved to cook! We spent a lot of time in the kitchen cooking, laughing, and learning about each other.

Sounds like the fairy tale story has arrived, right? Well, not so much you see, he had demons too that he hadn't dealt with either, so in the midst of our love there was a battle with our demons. We married each other, the year was 1974; I'll never forget that day. I made my own wedding dress, sewed the dresses of my bridesmaids too. My beautiful daughter walked down the aisle as my flower girl, my handsome son the ring bearer; it was a day for the storybooks.

Two years after we married, we had our first son together. I remember rubbing my belly while carrying him and asking God, "Please, let this one come out looking just like me." Silly request I know, but my other two children looked more like their father, I wanted one that looked just like me, and to my surprise he did. Joseph Leroy Poellnitz Jr. was born September 13, 1976, 8 pounds and 10 ounces; one of the happiest days of my life. We continued to live, now a family of 5 (my husband's two daughters resided with their mothers). My son fit right in, wreaking havoc on his older siblings who were 10 and 12 years older than him. To many we seemed perfect, in the right place; but we continued to shove those demons in the closet, not realizing they're multiplying.

In late 1977; with a one year old, 11 and 13 year old I found out I was pregnant again, but by this time life had gotten a hold of me. I had been drinking a lot prior to finding out I was pregnant; I turned to the drink to ease my pain. My husband struggled with a drug addiction he acquired while stationed in Vietnam. That war could have taken his life and before he allowed it take his mind he was determined to do whatever he needed to do to mask the pain. His goal was to avoid reliving that horrid time over in his head again and again.  His addiction affected us all.  I had children to think about; I couldn't let them fall prey to what his addiction could subject them too.  The pressure, when it became too much for me I drank.

The consequences of my drinking, even though I stopped as soon as I found out I was pregnant resulted in me prematurely delivering my next child.  On March 12, 1978 I gave birth to a baby girl; it was too soon, I was only 28 weeks at the time.  I wasn't even sure she would come out alive.  As soon as I delivered her, neonatal whisked her away to intensive care.  A while later doctors came back and gave me the prognosis, "Mrs. Poellnitz, she only weighs two pounds and eleven ounces, she's hooked up to a ventilator, she may not live long; we recommend you sign a release for us to not to resuscitate  should she stop breathing."  I politely looked at those doctors and in the sweetest tone I could, I told them, "Don't you dare give up on my daughter, and do all that you can to save her and what you cannot do God will."

God rescued me at every turn; I must've had great purpose because the enemy tried his best to destroy me and my family. My husband's struggles combined with my own was tough on my children. It was not fun seeing your father scrape up money for a hit or have your momma gather change to get a fifth. We weren't perfect, my husband and I but we did our best not to burden our crosses on the backs of our children. I'd learned to function drunk and my husband learned to operate while high, sounds crazy I know, but it's the truth. We went to church, we cooked for banquets, baked for baked sales and then God had enough.

God will not be mocked in anyone's life. You cannot Name drop Him when it's convenient for you; He's too Holy for that. God is the Almighty my husband and I had to learn that. Even in our learning He afforded us a measure of Grace that covered us. I accepted God's correction; when I did life turned around for me. I gave Him 100 percent and the life I craved at the beginning was finally coming true for me.

I learned the importance of time, how precious and priceless it is. I spent moments with my children, closed in my right mind. I instilled principles in them, prayed that God would cover and carry them through time. I believed greatness resided in each one of my children, so I was careful to speak life over them every chance I was given. I taught them about Jesus, His love, His grace, His forgiveness. I wanted to make sure my children understood the foundation of me, God the Father, Jesus the Son and the Holy Spirit.

I lived life more abundantly until the end of my life July 12, 1991. I was 44 years old when Jesus called me by my name. I died with honor, peacefully, no shame. The value of me shines strongly through my four children and I know God is carrying them just like He carried me.

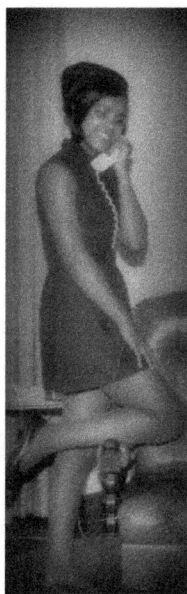

Rest In Peace
Juanita R. Poellnitz
February 17, 1947 – July 12, 1991


Gone But Not Forgotten

## Conclusion

It is my sincere hope that this book has encouraged, inspired, and empowered you as you read page by page. Every woman that contributed to this collection of work sacrificed to share intimate details of their lives; we thank you for taking time out to read this book.

To the contributors, I appreciate every single one of you! Thank you for your commitment to this book and your belief in the overall mission of I Am Valuable Mentoring Program™.

*Stacy C. Wilson,*

**Founder**, I Am Valuable Mentoring Program™.

*For More Information* about
**I Am Valuable Mentoring Program™** connect with us at:

[www.followinghisway.com](www.followinghisway.com)

Twitter:
@IAmValuableMent

Email Us:
[iamvaluablementoring@gmail.com](iamvaluablementoring@gmail.com)

Call Us: 678-856-7438

We'd LOVE to hear from you!!!